# High Quality Care For All

NHS Next Stage Review Final Report

Presented to Parliament
by the Secretary of State for Health
by Command of Her Majesty

June 2008

CM 7432

Gateway reference: 10106

# Introduction

In previous reviews of the NHS, frontline staff have been on the fringes or bystanders. This Review has been different. We and our colleagues in the NHS have been at its core. There has been an unprecedented opportunity for health and social care professionals to review the best available evidence, to discuss priorities with patients and the public, and develop compelling shared visions for our local NHS.

Through this Review, the NHS has created its own ambitious visions for the future of health and healthcare. This marks a real change in the relationship between the frontline NHS and the centre. Lord Darzi and the Department of Health have focused on supporting the improvements we want to make. This report will enable the local NHS to achieve what matters to us, to patients and to the public – improved health and high quality care for all.

**Dr James Cave**
**BSc (Hons) MBBS DRCOG FRCGP**
NHS South Central Clinical Lead
General Practitioner, Berkshire West
Primary Care Trust

**Professor Matthew Cooke**
**PhD FCEM FRCS (Ed)**
NHS West Midlands Clinical Lead
Professor of Emergency Medicine, Heart
of England NHS Foundation Trusts and
Warwick Medical School

**Sir Cyril Chantler**
**MA MD FRCP FRCPH FMedSci**
NHS London Clinical Lead
Chairman, Great Ormond Street Hospital
for Children NHS Trust

**Professor Peter Kelly**
**BSc PhD CStat FFPH**
NHS North East Clinical Lead
Executive Director of Public Health for
Tees Primary Care Trusts

**Professor Mayur Lakhani CBE**
FRCGP FRCP
NHS East Midlands Joint Clinical Lead
Medical Director, NHS East Midlands
Strategic Health Authority

**Dr Jonathan P Sheffield**
MBChB FRCPath
NHS South West Clinical Lead
Medical Director, University Hospitals
Bristol NHS Foundation Trust

**Dr Kathy McLean**
MBChB FRCP
NHS East Midlands Joint Clinical Lead
Medical Director, Derby Hospitals NHS
Foundation Trust

**Professor Christopher L Welsh**
MA MB MChir FRCS FFOM (Hon)
NHS Yorkshire and the Humber
Clinical Lead
Medical Director, Yorkshire and the
Humber Strategic Health Authority
and Chief Operating Officer, Sheffield
Teaching Hospitals NHS Foundation Trust

**Mr Edward Palfrey**
MA MB BChir FRCS FRCS(Ed)
NHS South East Coast Clinical Lead
Medical Director, Frimley Park Hospital
NHS Foundation Trust

**Dr Robert Winter**
MA MD FRCP
NHS East of England Clinical Lead
Medical Director, Cambridge University
Hospitals NHS Foundation Trust

**Dr Steve Ryan**
MBChB MD
NHS North West Clinical Lead
Medical Director Royal Liverpool
Children's NHS Trust

# Preface

By the Prime Minister

The National Health Service is not just a great institution but a unique and very British expression of an ideal – that healthcare is not a privilege to be purchased but a moral right secured for all.

For 60 years it has carried the support of the British people because it speaks to our values of fairness and opportunity for all and because it is always there for us when we are most vulnerable and in need.

That is why it is right that we should seek to renew the NHS for the 21st century. To meet the rising aspirations of the public, the changing burdens of disease and to ensure that the very latest, personalised healthcare is available to all of us, not just those able to pay.

Over the last 10 years we have improved the basic standards of the NHS. In 2000, the NHS Plan set out to tackle the challenges which chronic underinvestment had created. Since then we have invested in 80,000 more nurses and 38,000 more doctors, including 5,000 more GPs. Access to care has improved dramatically, and outcomes have improved as a result: 238,000 lives have been saved in the last 11 years as a result of significant improvements in cancer and heart disease survival rates in particular.

This report builds on those reforms and will, I believe, have an even more profound affect on NHS services and our experience of them. If the challenge 10 years ago was capacity, the challenge today is to drive improvements in the quality of care. We need a more personalised NHS, responsive to each of us as individuals, focused on prevention, better equipped to keep us healthy and capable of giving us real control and real choices over our care and our lives.

Lord Darzi's report is a tremendous opportunity to build an NHS that provides truly world class services for all. It requires Government to be serious about reform, committed to trusting frontline staff and ready to invest in new services and new ways of delivering services. It is a bold vision for an NHS which is among the best healthcare systems in the world – a once in a generation opportunity that we owe it to ourselves and our families to take.

I would like to thank Lord Darzi and the thousands of those who have been involved in the review locally and nationally for their contributions. As a Government the renewal of the NHS must be one of our very highest priorities and we will rise to the challenge you have set us.

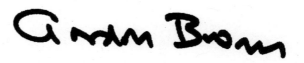

**Gordon Brown**
**Prime Minister**

# Foreword

By the Secretary of State for Health

On its 60th anniversary, the NHS is in good health.

The NHS touches our lives at times of basic human need, when care and compassion are what matter most. Over the past 60 years, it has been a vital friend to millions of people, sharing their joy and comforting their sorrow.

The service continues to be available to everyone, free at the point of need. One million people are seen or treated every 36 hours, and nine out of 10 people see their family doctor in any given year. In 2008, the NHS will carry out a million more operations than it did just 10 years ago.

Over the past decade, the NHS budget has trebled. It employs a third more people than it did – more doctors, more nurses, delivering better care for patients. We have invested in new facilities and advanced equipment – last autumn we announced an additional £250 million to improve access to GP services including over 100 new practices in the most deprived areas of the country.

The Prime Minister, Chancellor and I asked Lord Darzi to lead this Review working in partnership with patients, frontline staff and the public to develop a vision of a service fit for the 21st century. He has succeeded. The strength of this Review has been the 2,000 frontline clinicians and other local health and social care staff who have led the process, with thousands more staff, patients and members of the public involved across the country.

The NHS already delivers high quality care to patients in many respects. The NHS Next Stage Review makes a compelling case that it can deliver high quality care for patients in *all* respects. It is only because of the investment and reform of the past decade that this is now possible.

We are also launching an NHS Constitution for consultation. The NHS is as much a social movement as a health service. That is why it is so vital to secure its founding principles and set out the rights and responsibilities of patients, public and staff.

Lord Darzi has led this Review magnificently, bringing to bear huge personal credibility and integrity. I thank him and the thousands of people that have worked to create this Review locally and nationally. It is testament to what we can achieve when everyone in the NHS works together for the benefit of patients.

**The Rt Hon Alan Johnson MP**
**Secretary of State for Health**

# Contents

# Summary letter

Our NHS – Secured today for future generations
by Lord Darzi

*An NHS that gives patients and the public more information and choice, works in partnership and has quality of care at its heart.*

Dear Prime Minister, Chancellor of the Exchequer, and Secretary of State for Health,

This year the NHS is 60 years old. We are paying tribute to a service founded in adversity, from which were established enduring principles of equal access for all based on need and not ability to pay. We are celebrating a national institution that has made an immeasurable difference to millions of people's lives across the country.

Quite simply, the NHS is there when we need it most. It provides round the clock, compassionate care and comfort. It plays a vital role in ensuring that as many of us as possible can enjoy good health for as long as possible – one of the things that matters most to us and to our family and friends.

## The journey so far

I know the journey we have all been on from my own experience as an NHS clinician working in partnership with professional colleagues across the service.

I used to be the only colo-rectal surgeon in my hospital; today I am a member of a team of four surgeons, working in a network that reaches out into primary care. Ten years ago, we had one part-time stoma nurse. Today we have two full-time stoma nurses, two specialist nurses and a nurse consultant.

Ten years ago, my patients would sometimes wait over a year for treatment, and now they wait just a few weeks – and even less if cancer is suspected. My patients are treated using keyhole surgery enabling them to leave hospital in days rather than weeks. My team's conversations about quality take place in weekly multidisciplinary meetings rather than in corridors. Together, these changes have meant real improvements for patients.

I have seen for myself the NHS getting better, and I have heard similar stories from other clinical teams throughout the country over the course of this Review. These achievements were enabled by the investment of extra resources,[1] by giving freedom to the frontline through NHS foundation trusts, and by ensuring more funding followed patient choices. They were delivered by the dedication and hard work of NHS staff who were determined to improve services for patients and the public.

---

1   In 1996/7, the budget for the NHS in England was £33 billion; in 2008/9 it is £96 billion.

## The next stage of the journey

My career is dedicated to improving continuously the quality of care we provide for patients. This is what inspires me and my professional colleagues, and it has been the guiding principle for this Review. We need to continue the NHS journey of improvements and move from an NHS that has rightly focused on increasing the quantity of care to one that focuses on improving the quality of care.

There is still much more to do to achieve this. I have continued my clinical practice while leading the Review nationally. I have seen and treated patients every week. Maintaining that personal connection with patients has helped me understand the improvements we still need to make. It has driven me to focus this Review on practical action.

It is because of this that I have been joined in this Review by 2,000 clinicians and other health and social care professionals from every NHS region in England. Their efforts, in considering the best available evidence and in setting out their own visions for high quality services (described in *Chapter 1*), have been the centrepiece of this process.

Their visions – developed in discussion with patients, carers and members of the general public – set out bold and ambitious plans. I am excited by the local leadership they demonstrate and the commitment of all those who have been involved.

In developing the visions, the NHS has had to face up to significant variations in the quality of care that is provided.

Tackling this will be our first priority. The NHS needs to be flexible to respond to the needs of local communities, but people need to be confident that standards are high across the board.

Delivering the visions will mean tackling head on those variations in the quality of care and giving patients more information and choice. The message they send is that the programme of reform that has been put in place has been unevenly applied and can go much further.

We also need to accelerate change for other reasons. *Chapter 2* describes the changes facing society and healthcare systems around the world. It sets out how the NHS in the 21st century faces a particular set of challenges, which I would summarise as: rising expectations; demand driven by demographics; the continuing development of our 'information society'; advances in treatments; the changing nature of disease; and changing expectations of the health workplace. These are challenges we cannot avoid. The NHS should anticipate and respond to the challenges of the future.

My conclusions, and the measures described in this report, focus on how we can accelerate the changes that frontline staff want to make to meet those challenges, whilst continuing to raise standards.

The vision this report sets out is of an NHS that gives patients and the public more information and choice, works in partnership and has quality of care at its heart – quality defined as clinically effective, personal and safe. It will see the NHS deliver high quality care for all users of services in all aspects, not just some. I set out below the key steps we must take to deliver this vision.

## High quality care for patients and the public

Throughout this Review, I have heard clearly and consistently that people want a greater degree of control and influence over their health and healthcare. If anything, this is even more important for those who for a variety of reasons find it harder to seek out services or make themselves heard.

Personalising services means making services fit for everyone's needs, not just those of the people who make the loudest demands. When they need it, all patients want care that is personal to them.[2] That includes those people traditionally less likely to seek help or who find themselves discriminated against in some way. The visions published in each NHS region make clear that more support is needed for all people to help them stay healthy and particularly to improve the health of those most in need. *Chapter 3* explains how we will do this including by introducing new measures to:

**Create an NHS that helps people to stay healthy**. For the NHS to be sustainable in the 21st century it needs to focus on improving health as well as treating sickness. This is not about the 'nanny state'. As a clinician, I believe that the NHS has a responsibility to promote good health as well as tackle illness.

Achieving this goal requires the NHS to work in partnership with the many other agencies that also seek to promote health. Much progress on closer working has been made in recent years. In line with my terms of reference,[3] this reports focuses on what the NHS can do to improve the prevention of ill health.

The immediate steps identified by this Review are:

- **Every primary care trust will commission comprehensive wellbeing and prevention services, in partnership with local authorities, with the services offered personalised to meet the specific needs of their local populations**. Our efforts must be focused on six key goals: tackling obesity, reducing alcohol harm, treating drug addiction, reducing smoking rates, improving sexual health and improving mental health.

- **A Coalition for Better Health, with a set of new voluntary agreements between the Government, private and third sector organisations on actions to improve health outcomes**. Focused initially on combatting obesity, the Coalition will be based on agreements to ensure healthier food, to get more people more physically active, and to encourage companies to invest more in the health of their workforce.

---

2   Opinion Leader Research, Key findings of 18 September 2007 *Our NHS, Our Future* nationwide consultative event.

3   Terms of Reference available at www.ournhs.nhs.uk

- **Raised awareness of vascular risk assessment through a new 'Reduce Your Risk' campaign**. As we roll out the new national programme of vascular risk assessment for people aged between 40 and 74, we will raise awareness through a nationwide 'Reduce Your Risk' campaign – helping people to stay healthy and to know when they need to get help.

- **Support for people to stay healthy at work**. We will introduce integrated Fit for Work services, to help people who want to return to work but are struggling with ill health to get back to appropriate work faster.

- **Support GPs to help individuals and their families stay healthy**. We will work with world-leading professionals and patient groups to improve the Quality and Outcomes Framework to provide better incentives for maintaining good health as well as good care.

We will give patients more rights and control over their own health and care. I have heard the need to give patients more information and choice to make the system more responsive to their personal needs. We will:

- **Extend choice of GP practice**. Patients will have greater choice of GP practice and better information to help them choose. We will develop a fairer funding system, ensuring better rewards for GPs who provide responsive, accessible and high quality services. The NHS Choices website will provide more information about all primary and community care services, so that people can make informed choices.

- **Introduce a new right to choice in the first NHS Constitution**. The draft NHS Constitution includes rights to choose both treatment and providers and to information on quality, so that, wherever it is relevant to them, patients are able to make informed choices.

- **Ensure everyone with a long-term condition has a personalised care plan**. Care plans will be agreed by the patient and a named professional and provide a basis for the NHS and its partners to organise services around the needs of individuals.

- **Pilot personal health budgets**. Learning from experience in social care and other health systems, personal health budgets will be piloted, giving individuals and families greater control over their own care, with clear safeguards. We will pilot direct payments where this makes most sense for particular patients in certain circumstances.

- **Guarantee patients access to the most clinically and cost effective drugs and treatments**. All patients will receive drugs and treatments approved by the National Institute for Health and Clinical Excellence (NICE) where the clinician recommends them. NICE appraisals processes will be speeded up.

The common theme of these new measures for patients is improving quality. It must be the basis of everything we do in the NHS.

## Quality at the heart of the NHS

In my career as a surgeon, I try to do my best to provide patients with high quality NHS care – just like hundreds of thousands of other staff. This has been my guiding principle as I have led this Review.

High quality care should be as safe and effective as possible, with patients treated with compassion, dignity and respect. As well as clinical quality and safety, quality means care that is personal to each individual.

As independent research has shown,[4] the NHS has made good progress over the past decade in improving the overall quality of care for patients. During this period, improvements in quality were focused primarily on waiting times, as basic acceptable standards of access to A&E and secondary care were established, and on staffing levels and physical infrastructure.

Today, with the NHS budget approaching £2 billion a week, more staff, and improvements in the quality and availability of information, quality can be at the heart of everything we do in the NHS. It means moving from high quality care in some aspects to high quality care in all.

We will raise standards. The visions set out for each NHS region and formed by patients' expectations are ambitious for what the NHS can achieve. *Chapter 4* of this report sets out the measures that will enable us to meet these standards:

- **Getting the basics right first time, every time**. We will continue to seek improvements in safety and reductions in healthcare associated infections. The Care Quality Commission will have new enforcement powers. There will be national campaigns to make care even safer.

- **Independent quality standards and clinical priority setting**. NICE will be expanded to set and approve more independent quality standards. A new National Quality Board will offer transparent advice to Ministers on what the priorities should be for clinical standard setting by NICE.

- **For the first time we will systematically measure and publish information about the quality of care from the frontline up**. Measures will include patients' own views on the success of their treatment and the quality of their experiences. There will also be measures of safety and clinical outcomes. All registered healthcare providers working for, or on behalf of, the NHS will be required by law to publish 'Quality Accounts' just as they publish financial accounts.

---

4    S Leatherman and K Sutherland, *The Quest for Quality: Refining the NHS Reforms*, Nuffield Trust, May 2008 and K Davis et al., *Mirror, Mirror on the Wall: An international update on the comparative performance of American healthcare*, Commonwealth Fund, May 2007.

- **Making funding for hospitals that treat NHS patients reflect the quality of care that patients receive**. For the first time, patients' own assessments of the success of their treatment and the quality of their experiences will have a direct impact on the way hospitals are funded.

- **For senior doctors, the current Clinical Excellence Awards Scheme will be strengthened, to reinforce quality improvement**. New awards, and the renewal of existing awards, will become more conditional on clinical activity and quality indicators; and the Scheme will encourage and support clinical leadership of service delivery and innovation.

- **Easy access for NHS staff to information about high quality care**. All NHS staff will have access to a new NHS Evidence service where they will be able to get, through a single web-based portal, authoritative clinical and non-clinical evidence and best practice.

- **Measures to ensure continuous improvement in the quality of primary and community care**. We have just completed our consultation on proposals to bring all GP practices and dental practices within the scope of the new health and adult social care regulator, the Care Quality Commission.[5] We will introduce a new strategy for developing the Quality and Outcomes Framework which will include an independent and

transparent process for developing and reviewing indicators. We will support practice accreditation schemes, like that of the Royal College of General Practitioners.

- Developing **new best practice tariffs focused on areas for improvement**. These will pay for best practice rather than average cost, meaning NHS organisations will need to improve to keep up.

We will strengthen the involvement of clinicians in decision making at every level of the NHS. As this Review has shown, change is most likely to be effective if it is led by clinicians. We will do this by ensuring that:

- **Medical directors and quality boards feature at regional and national level.** These will complement the arrangements at PCT level that are developing as part of the World Class Commissioning programme.

- **Strategic plans for delivering the visions will be published later this year by every primary care trust**. Change will be based on the five principles I set out earlier this year in *Leading Local Change*.[6]

- There is clear **local support for quality improvement**. A new 'Quality Observatory' will be established in every NHS region to inform local quality improvement efforts.

---

5   Department of Health, *The future regulation of health and adult social in England*, 25 March 2008.

6   *NHS Next Stage Review: Leading Local Change*, Department of Health, May 2008.

We will foster a pioneering NHS. Throughout my career, in all the clinical teams I have worked in, my colleagues and I have challenged one another to improve the way we provide care for patients. Continuous advances in clinical practice mean the NHS constantly has the opportunity to improve. My review will enable this through:

- **Introducing new responsibilities, funds and prizes to support and reward innovation.** Strategic health authorities will have a new legal duty to promote innovation. New funds and prizes will be available to the local NHS.

- **Ensuring that clinically and cost effective innovation in medicines and medical technologies is adopted**. We will strengthen the horizon scanning process for new medicines in development, involving industry systematically to support better forward planning and develop ways to measure uptake. For new medical technologies, we will simplify the pathway by which they pass from development into wider use, and develop ways to benchmark and monitor uptake.

- **Creating new partnerships between the NHS, universities and industry.** These 'clusters' will enable pioneering new treatments and models of care to be developed and then delivered directly to patients.

These changes will help the NHS to provide high quality care across the board. Throughout this Review, it has been clear that high quality care cannot be mandated from the centre – it requires the unlocking of the talents of frontline staff.

## Working in partnership with staff

I have heard some people claim that there is 'change fatigue' in the NHS. I understand that NHS staff are tired of upheaval – when change is driven top-down. It is for this reason that I chose to make this Review primarily local, led by clinicians and other staff working in the NHS and partner organisations. In my own practice and across the country I have seen that, where change is led by clinicians and based on evidence of improved quality of care, staff who work in the NHS are energised by it and patients and the public more likely to support it.

We will empower frontline staff to lead change that improves quality of care for patients. *Chapter 5* sets out how we will do this by:

- **Placing a new emphasis on enabling NHS staff to lead and manage the organisations in which they work**. We will re-invigorate practice-based commissioning and give greater freedoms and support to high performing GP practices to develop new services for their patients, working with other primary and community clinicians. We will provide more integrated services for patients, by piloting new integrated care organisations, bringing together health and social care professionals from a range of organisations – community services, hospitals, local authorities and others, depending on local needs.

- **Implementing wide ranging programme to support the development of vibrant, successful community health services**. Where PCTs and staff choose to set up social enterprise organisations, transferred staff can continue to benefit from the NHS Pension Scheme while they work wholly on NHS funded work. We will also encourage and enable staff to set up social enterprises by introducing a 'staff right to request' to set up social enterprises to deliver services.

- **Enhancing professionalism**. There will be investment in new programmes of clinical and board leadership, with clinicians encouraged to be practitioners, partners and leaders in the NHS. We challenge *all* organisations that do business as part of, or with, the NHS to give clinicians more control over budgets and HR decisions.

- **No new national targets** are set in this report.

We will value the work of NHS staff. NHS staff make the difference where it matters most and we have an obligation to patients and the public to enable them to make best use of their talents. That is why the Review announces in *Chapter 6*:

- **New pledges to staff**. The NHS Constitution makes pledges on work and wellbeing, learning and development, and involvement and

partnership. All NHS organisations will have a statutory duty to have regard to the Constitution.

- **A clear focus on improving the quality of NHS education and training**. The system will be reformed in partnership with the professions.

- **A threefold increase in investment in nurse and midwife preceptorships**. These offer protected time for newly qualified nurses and midwives to learn from their more senior colleagues during their first year.

- **Doubling investment in apprenticeships**. Healthcare support staff – clinical and non-clinical – are the backbone of the service. Their learning and development will be supported through more apprenticeships.

- **Strengthened arrangements to ensure staff have consistent and equitable opportunities to update and develop their skills**. Sixty per cent of staff who will deliver NHS services in 10 years time are already working in healthcare.We need to make sure that they are able to keep their skills and knowledge up to date.

### The first NHS Constitution

You asked me to consider the case for an NHS Constitution. In *Chapter 7*, I set out why I believe it will be a powerful way to secure the defining features of the service for the next generation. I have heard that whilst changes must be made to improve quality, the best of the NHS, the values and core principles which underpin it, must be protected and enshrined. An NHS Constitution will help patients by setting out, for the first time, the extensive set of legal rights they already have in relation to the NHS. It will ensure that decision-making is local where possible and more accountable than it is today, providing clarity and transparency about who takes what decisions on our behalf.

Finally, *Chapter 8* sets out how we will deliver this ambitious programme.

## Conclusion

In the 21<sup>st</sup> century, there remains a compelling case for a tax-funded, free at the point of need, National Health Service. This Report celebrates its successes, describes where there is clear room for improvement, looks forward to a bright future, and seeks to secure it for generations to come through the first NHS Constitution. The focus on prevention, improved quality and innovation will support the NHS in its drive to ensure the best possible value for money for taxpayers. It is also an excellent opportunity to pursue our duties to promote equality and reduce discrimination under the Equality and Human Rights Act.

Through this process, we have developed a shared diagnosis of where we currently are, a unified vision of where we want to be and a common language framework to help us get there. This Review has built strong foundations for the future of the service. It outlines the shape of the next stage of reform, with the clarity and flexibility to give confidence for the future.

Leadership will make this change happen. All of the 2,000 frontline staff that have led this Review have shown themselves to be leaders by having the courage to step up and make the case for change. Their task has only just begun – it is relatively easy to set out a vision, much harder to make it a reality. As they strive to make change happen, they can count on my full support.

I would like to thank everyone who has participated in this Review. I am grateful for the help they have given to me in forming and shaping the conclusions of this Report.

Best wishes,

**Professor the Lord Darzi
of Denham KBE**
**Hon FREng, FMedSci**
*Parliamentary Under Secretary of State*

Paul Hamlyn Chair of Surgery,
Imperial College London
Honorary Consultant Surgeon,
Imperial College Healthcare NHS Trust
and the Royal Marsden Hospital
NHS Foundation Trust

# 1

# Change – locally-led, patient-centred and clinically driven

A nationwide process – the core of the
NHS Next Stage Review

An emergency care practitioner from
the Cornwall Ambulance Service
responds to a call in Port Quin, Cornwall

# 1

# Change – locally-led, patient-centred and clinically driven

A nationwide process – the core of the NHS Next Stage Review

1. The challenge for this Review, set out in my terms of reference, was to "help local patients, staff and the public in making the changes they need and want for their local NHS."[7] This approach was necessary because change is best when it is determined locally. Changing well-loved services can be unsettling for patients, public and staff. Therefore, it is important that the local NHS goes through a proper process to determine what will work best, involving patients, carers, the general public and staff, whilst communicating clearly throughout.

2. This has meant a very different type of Review, one driven by the NHS itself. Over the past few months, each region of the NHS has published its vision for improving health and healthcare services.

3. These visions are the product of the work more than 2,000 clinicians and other staff in health and social care, who have shown tremendous leadership in creating, shaping and forming the conclusions. In each region, they have met in eight or more groups reflecting different 'pathways of care' – from maternity and newborn care through to end of life care.[8] These groups have considered the best available clinical evidence, worked in partnership with thousands of patients, listened to the needs and aspirations of the public and set out comprehensive and coherent visions for the future.

4. The visions are the centrepiece of this Review – they report much progress, but also identify where, based on clinical evidence, further change is required in order to provide high quality care. They show how the NHS is responding to people's needs throughout their lives, from before birth, through childhood and adolescence and into adulthood and old age. They describe the priorities for action and explain what difference these priorities, once implemented, will make for local populations.

5. The proposals will allow NHS services everywhere to reflect the needs of their local communities. People and communities across England have different characteristics and different needs. Yet too often, the services they receive are not sufficiently shaped around those characteristics and needs. If the NHS is to live up

---

7   The terms of reference are available at www.ournhs.nhs.uk

8   Some of the strategic health authorities chose to create more than eight groups. South West SHA for instance had a group looking at the best care for people with learning disabilities

1

to its founding principles, it must constantly respond to those it serves, changing to continue to live up to the ambition of high quality care. The NHS should be universal, but that does not mean that it should be uniform. Clear minimum standards and entitlements will exist, but not a one size fits all model.

6. These visions are the start of responding to local needs. They describe an NHS that will work with partner organisations locally to reach out and help people stay healthy, and, when people do need care, provide convenient, high quality care. Services will be found in the community, with family doctors, pharmacies and local partnerships taking a leading role in helping people to stay healthy. In future, the NHS will not be confined to hospitals, health centres or GP surgeries but will be available online and in people's homes, whilst the most specialist care will be concentrated to allow excellence to flourish.

7. Although the specific steps in each region's vision varied as the clinical working groups found the best solutions for their local populations, their reports include some important common messages:

- The **staying healthy** groups identified the need to support people to take responsibility for their own health, through reaching out to disadvantaged groups. They also highlighted the expansion of comprehensive screening and immunisation programmes.

- The **maternity and newborn** groups were clear that women want high quality, personal care with greater choice over place of birth, and care provided by a named midwife.

- For the **children's** pathway, it was felt that services need to be more effectively designed around the needs of children and families, delivered not just in health settings but also in schools and children's centres.

- The **acute care** groups gave compelling arguments for saving lives by creating specialised centres for major trauma, heart attack and stroke care, supported by skilled ambulance services.

- Those looking at **planned care** found more care could, and should, be provided closer to people's homes, with greater use of technology, and outpatient care not always meaning a trip to hospital.

- For **mental health**, the groups recognised the importance of extending services in the community, and the benefits to general wellbeing and to physical from stronger mental health promotion.

- The **long-term conditions** groups explained the need for true partnerships between people with long-term conditions and the professionals and volunteers that care for them, underpinned by care plans and better patient information.

- The necessity for greater dignity and respect at the **end of life** was movingly described by the end of life groups, as well as the desire to have round the clock access to palliative services.

8. It is impossible to do justice here to the breadth of ambition within the local visions – they demand to be read.[9] However, we can illustrate important themes with specific local promises.

### Preventing ill health

9. There is a clear consensus across the service that the NHS must help people to lead independent and fulfilling lives by supporting them to stay healthy. The local NHS wants to work with others to help people stop smoking, to address obesity in children and adults, and to tackle excessive alcohol consumption. In the East of England, for example, patients, the public and staff have set themselves the ambition of reducing the number of smokers in their region by 140,000, from its current level of a million.[10]

They are developing plans for a social marketing campaign to encourage people to take responsibility for their own health throughout their lives, whilst reaching out to the most disadvantaged in society to help them to stay healthy.

### Ensuring timely access

10. There was a strong message that people can still find it difficult to access services. Improving access is a priority articulated in every vision, across every pathway of care. Each region will continue to improve the quality of access by reducing waiting times for treatment, whilst ensuring that services are available regardless of where a patient lives. The plans to improve dementia services in the West Midlands, and South Central's goal to deliver round the clock palliative care for children, are just two of the many examples where the local NHS will transform access to services for patients.[11]

### Providing convenient care closer to home

11. The local visions will make care closer to home a reality for many patients. For instance, in London, there are plans to deliver more outpatient appointments in community settings and carry out routine and straightforward procedures in GP practices, where appropriate.[12]

---

9   The local visions are available at www.ournhs.nhs.uk

10  NHS East of England, *Towards the best, together*, May 2008.

11  NHS West Midlands, *Delivering Our Clinical Vision for a World Class Health Service*, June 2008 and NHS South Central, *Towards a Healthier Future*, June 2008.

12  NHS London, *Healthcare for London: A Framework for Action*, July 2007.

1

NHS North West is making specialist knowledge more locally available through the use of cardiac telemedicine in GP practices.[13] This allows GPs to make a diagnosis, with the help of specialists at the end of a phone, in their own surgeries.

## Improved diagnostics

12. All the visions emphasised the importance of rapid access to diagnostics in convenient locations.[14] On the one hand, this means tests such as x-rays and blood tests carried out in primary care or even at patients' homes, avoiding needless travel to and from hospital and with results made available more quickly. On the other, it means provision of interventional radiology and specialist pathology in centres of excellence. To make this a reality, it will be important to take into account Lord Carter's review of pathology services[15] and draw on the expertise of professional bodies.

## Giving more control to patients

13. The NHS locally is seeking to forge a new partnership between professionals, patients and their carers. NHS North East, for example, is searching for new ways to integrate care around the needs of patients, including community services.[16] There will be more use of assistive technology and remote monitoring to help patients lead independent lives. It is suggested that patients should have more direct control over NHS spending – for instance, NHS Yorkshire and the Humber has called for the consideration of personal budgets for people with complex long-term conditions.[17]

## Ensuring care is effective and safe

14. The visions have sent a powerful message that the most effective treatments should be available for all NHS patients. Their plans for transforming treatment for heart attack, stroke and major trauma vividly illustrate this. For stroke – the third largest cause of death and single largest cause of disability in the UK – the clinical evidence clearly demonstrates that the quality of care is greatly improved if stroke is treated in specialist centres.[18] Each region is therefore pushing forward with the development of specialised centres for their populations with access to 24/7 brain imaging and thrombolysis delivered by expert teams. For example, by 2010, NHS South East Coast intends that all strokes, heart attacks and major injuries will be treated in such specialist centres.[19] Once implemented, these plans will save lives. From every corner of the NHS, there was also a strong emphasis on the importance of patient safety. They all aim to make hospitals and health centres clean and as free of infection as possible.

13 NHS North West, *Healthier Horizons*, May 2008.
14 See for instance, NHS West Midlands, *Delivering Our Clinical Vision for a World Class Health Service*, June 2008.
15 Lord Carter, *Report of the Review of NHS Pathology Services in England*, 2006.
16 NHS North East, *Our vision, our future*, June 2008.
17 NHS Yorkshire and the Humber, *Healthier Ambitions*, May 2008.
18 A. Buchan, Best practice in Stroke Care 2007, presentation at the Healthcare for London conference, 19 February 2007.
19 NHS South East Coast, *Healthier People, Excellent Care*, June 2008.

15. The visions also emphasise the importance of geographical factors in the effectiveness and safety of care. This was reinforced by a submission report to this Review by the Commission for Rural Communities.[20]

## High quality care

16. From the vision documents, and from my own visits to every region of the country, the message that improving quality of care is what excites and energises NHS staff has been loud and clear. International evidence shows that we have made great improvements but that there is further to go. Nolte and McKee have found that the NHS made a 21 per cent reduction in premature mortality rates from 1997–98 to 2002–03, compared to a 4 per cent reduction by the US.[21] However, there is much more to do, as our starting point was worse than our international comparators.

17. Every region of the NHS has articulated its aspiration for high quality care for their populations. NHS South West, for example, has set a goal of matching the longest life expectancy in Europe.[22] Using clinical expertise, NHS East Midlands will publish standard quality measures allowing patients to compare the performance of different providers.[23]

## Personal care

18. All the visions emphasised the need to organise care around the individual, meeting their needs not just clinically, but also in terms of dignity and respect. NHS South West, for instance, recognised that the best diabetes services are tailored to individuals, comprising a mix of structured education, lifestyle advice and appropriate screening.[24] Personal care also considers the needs of the patient within the context of their support network, including carers, family and employers.

## Innovation

19. The desire to bring the benefits of innovation to patients more rapidly is a common theme. Across the country, from the South West to the North East, we heard that there is much to be gained by the NHS working in partnership with higher education institutions and the private sector. And there is very strong support for greater collaboration between primary, secondary and social care.

20. These are the changes patients and public can expect to see. However, there was one more common theme – all the local visions made the case for national action to enable local change. This report therefore sets out how we will help the local NHS to ensure that the pace of change does not slow and that the expectations of patients and the public are met. It describes how we will respond to the challenges the visions set, helping patients, the public and frontline staff to achieve their collective ambitions.

20 Commission for Rural Communities, *Tackling rural disadvantages*, May 2008
21 E. Nolte and N. McKee, "Measuring the Health of Nations, updating an earlier analysis, 2008," *Health Affairs* 27:10, 58–71.
22 NHS South West, *Improving Health*, May 2008.
23 NHS East Midlands, *From Evidence to Excellence*, June 2008.

24 NHS South West, *Improving Health*, May 2008.

1

21. This report addresses big national themes such as improving quality, leadership and the workforce.[25] It focuses on what must be done centrally to support local organisations. It illustrates that the role of the Department of Health is to enable the visions created by the local NHS to become a reality, whilst ensuring that universality, minimum standards and entitlements are retained and strengthened. It sets out how we will back local leaders to deliver for their communities.

25 National Groups were established as part of the Review in October 2007 on Quality and Safety, Leadership, Primary and Community Care, Workforce, and Innovation.

# 2
# Changes in healthcare and society
The challenges facing the NHS in the 21st century

A patient undergoes plasma exchange at the Royal Liverpool Hospital

# 2

# Changes in healthcare and society

The challenges facing the NHS in the 21st century

1. Every SHA vision identified the challenges faced in their region of the country.[26] Drawing together the common themes, it is possible to take a national perspective. The drivers for change in healthcare and society are beyond the control of any single organisation. Nor can they be dealt with simply or reactively at national level. This reinforces the case for enabling and encouraging the NHS locally to anticipate and respond proactively to the challenges of the future.

2. In its earliest years, the NHS faced significant challenges to provide basic care when people fell sick and to tackle communicable diseases. Nowadays, diseases such as measles, polio and diphtheria, previously common and deadly to the post-war generation, are rare and preventable, thanks to vaccination programmes, and treatable, thanks to advances in research and technology.

3. Nationally, the NHS in the 21st century faces different challenges, which I would summarise as: rising expectations; demand driven by demographics; the continuing development of our 'information society'; advances in treatments;

the changing nature of disease; and changing expectations of the health workplace.

4. These six challenges are not limited to England – they are common to all advanced health systems, most of which are considering or undertaking significant reforms in response.[27] Not all the challenges are unique to healthcare – their impact is being felt across public services. The Government is committed to transforming adult social care, for example, so that people have more choice and control over integrated, high quality services.[28] In addressing these challenges for the NHS we have the opportunity to set a direction for wider public service reform.

## Challenge 1: Ever higher expectations

5. Wealth and technology have changed the nature of our society's outlook and expectations. The 1942 Beveridge Report[29] identified the 'Five Giants' – want, disease, ignorance, squalor and idleness – that a civilised

---

26 See for instance *Healthcare for London the Case for Change.*

27 For an influential examination of the need to reform the US health system see Porter and Teisberg, *Redefining Health Care*, 2006.

28 *Putting People First, A shared vision and commitment to the transformation of adult social care*, HM Government, December 2007.

29 *Report of the Inter-Departmental Committee on Social Insurance and Allied Services*, Crown Copyright (1942).

2

society needed collectively to address. In 1946, the Labour government legislated for the creation of a National Health Service, and through the leadership of Nye Bevan the NHS was born on 5 July 1948. As an information leaflet from the time explained, its purpose was simple: to "relieve your money worries in time of illness."[30]

6. We tend to use health services at particular stages of our lives, so health professionals are especially exposed to each generation's demands and expectations. We can anticipate these changing demands, and in so doing equip the health service to deal with the future.

7. For those in later life, health practitioners will see a generation with expectations of more tailored treatment received at a time and place convenient to them. As people continue to live longer, they will continue to access services for longer, and are likely to live more of their life with one or more long-term condition.[31] They will make demands that are not just larger but different. They still expect the clinician to lead, but expect a bigger role for themselves in decision-making during their care.

8. We are also beginning to see the impact, and opportunities, that face us from recent generations – the children of the last three decades of the 20th century. These generations are influenced by new technologies that provide unprecedented levels of control, personalisation and connection. They expect not just services that are there when they need them, and treat them how they want them to, but that they can influence and shape for themselves. Better still, they will want services that 'instinctively' respond to them using the sophisticated marketing techniques used by other sectors.[32] This is more than just a challenge for healthcare, but for our whole model of how we think about *health*.

## Challenge 2: Demand driven by demographics

9. The fact that people are living longer than ever is a cause for celebration. The NHS can be justly proud of the part it has played in our ever-growing life expectancy. Yet our ageing population also poses a challenge to the sustainability of the NHS. By 2031, the number of over 75 year-olds in the British population will increase from 4.7 million to 8.2 million.[33] This older age group uses a disproportionate amount of NHS resources; the average over-85 year old is 14 times more likely to be admitted to hospital for medical reasons than the average 15-39

30  *The New National Health Service*, Central Office of Information for the Ministry of Health, Crown Copyright (1948).

31  See Wanless, *Securing our Future Health* (2002) for an explanation on how the NHS must not simply help people live longer, but must also ensure that those extra years are active, high quality ones.

32  For instance the personal recommendations given by Amazon and other internet retailers.

33  Office of National Statistics, *Population Projections*, 23 October 2007.

year old.[34] Whilst just 17 per cent of the under 40s have a long-term condition, 60 per cent of the 65 and over age group suffer from one or more.[35]

10. If the NHS remains a primarily reactive service, simply admitting people into hospital when they are ill, it will be unable to cope with the increased demands of an ageing population. Our longer life spans require the NHS to be forward-looking, proactively identifying and mitigating health risks.

## Challenge 3: Health in an age of information and connectivity

11. Across society, the internet has transformed our relationship with information. High-speed web access is found in millions of homes. By 2012, 74 per cent of UK homes are expected to have broadband internet access, transforming how people will seek and use information in their lives.[36]

12. The implications for health and healthcare are profound. It is easier to access information on how to stay healthy than ever before. People are able to quickly and conveniently find information about treatment and diseases in a way that was previously impossible. They are able, and want, to engage with others online, sharing information and experiences. They want to do their own research, reflect on what their clinicians have told them and discuss issues from an informed position. The challenge is ensuring that people are able to access reliable information. Evidence shows that clinicians have sometimes been slower in exploiting the potential of new information sources, such as the internet, than others.[37] If that trend continues, there is a danger that people will have to navigate through myth and hearsay, rather than get easy access to evidence-based medical knowledge.

## Challenge 4: The changing nature of disease

13. The NHS in the 21st century increasingly faces a disease burden determined by the choices people make: to smoke, drink excessively, eat poorly, and not take enough exercise. Today, countless years of healthy life are lost as the result of these known behavioural or lifestyle factors.

14. Wealth and technology have given us many choices, including ones that are damaging to our health and wellbeing. We drive to work and school instead of walking or cycling; we eat high fat, high salt diets when fresh fruit and vegetables are available in unprecedented volumes; and we consume more alcohol than is good for us.[38]

34 Hospital Episode Statistics Data 2005/06.

35 Department of Health, *Raising the Profile of Long-term Conditions: A Compendium of Information*, January 2008.

36 UK Broadband Overview, January 2008, http://point-topic.com/content/operatorSource/profiles2/uk-broadband-overview.htm

37 Kaimal AJ et al. "Google Obstetrics: who is educating our patients?" *American Journal of Obstetrics and Gynecology*, June 2008, 198(6):682.e1-5.

38 In the ten years to 2003, the number of walking trips fell by 20% (National Statistics 2004). The average number of cycling journeys fell from 20 person per year in 1992/1994 to 16 in 2002/2003 (DfT). 1 in 4 adults (10 million) regularly exceed the recommended daily limits of 2-3 units (women) and 3-4 units (men) (ONS General Household Survey 2006).

2

15. We know that the choices people make when faced with this increasing range of possibilities are strongly influenced by their circumstances. Stress, income, employment prospects and environmental factors constrain the healthy choices open to people, and can make short-term choices more attractive despite adverse health consequences in the longer term. The health service is not always good enough at helping people make the right choices – 54 per cent of patients said that their GP had not provided advice on diet and exercise, whilst 72 per cent said that their GP had not asked about emotional issues affecting their health during the last two years. We lag behind our peers internationally.[39]

16. Unhealthy choices and missed prevention opportunities are in part the cause of the growth in the prevalence of conditions such as diabetes, depression, and chronic obstructive pulmonary disease. The WHO estimates that depression, for instance, will be second only to HIV/AIDS as a contributor to the global burden of disease by 2030, up from fourth place today.[40] These diseases cannot always be cured, but they can be managed, and the symptoms ameliorated.

17. The NHS and all of its many partners must respond to this shifting disease burden and provide personalised care for long-term conditions, a goal already set out in the Government's *Our health, our care, our say* White Paper.[41] We need to make this goal a reality. Providing personalised care should also help us to reduce health inequalities, as the households with the lowest incomes are most likely to contain a member with a long-term condition.[42]

## Challenge 5: Advances in treatments

18. The past 60 years have seen big developments in our capacity to understand the nature and impact of existing disease, from imaging to pathology. We are improving our understanding of how disease in one organ increases the risk of damage to others. With the advances currently underway in genomic testing, we may be able to predict future disease rather than simply understand present illness.[43] Advances in neurosciences are telling us more about the importance of pregnancy and early childhood for subsequent health and wellbeing.[44] Our understanding of the wider determinants of physical and

39 2006 Commonwealth Fund international Health Policy Survey of Primary Care Physicians.

40 This is based on the impact of depression of Disability Adjusted Life Years (DALYs). C. Mathers and D. Loncar, Projections of Global Mortality and Burden from Disease 2002 to 2030, *PLoS Med* 3(11): e442.

41 *Our health, our care, our say,* HM Government, January 2006.

42 Department of Health, *Raising the Profile of long-term Conditions: A Compendium of Information,* January 2008.

43 K Philips et al, "Genetic testing and pharmacogenomics: issues for determining the impact to healthcare delivery and costs," *Am J of Managed Care,* 2004 Jul; 10(7): 425-432.

44 Center on the Developing Child at Harvard University (2007) *A Science-based framework for early childhood policy: using evidence to improve outcomes in learning, behaviour and health for vulnerable children* Cambridge, MA.

mental health and their impact and interactions is improving all the time. All of this presents the NHS with an unprecedented opportunity to move from reactive diagnosis and treatment to be able to proactively predict and prevent ill health.

19. Improved technology is enabling patients that would once have been hospitalised to live fulfilling lives in the community, supported by their family doctor and multi-professional community teams. Where patients were once confined to hospital, Wireless and Bluetooth technologies allow their health to be monitored in their own homes. For instance, a thousand people in Cornwall are having simple-to-use biometric equipment installed in their own homes, enabling them to monitor their own blood pressure, blood sugar and blood oxygen levels.[45] This information helps to prevent unnecessary hospital admissions. This is better for patients and their carers, delivers improved outcomes, and is a very efficient way of using NHS resources. An even bigger factor in the shift from hospital to home is the up-skilling of a wider range of staff, and the removal of barriers to more independent working in the patient's interest.

20. We continue to develop pioneering treatments for diseases. For the same illness, open surgery leaves patients in hospital for several weeks where keyhole surgery enables them to go home in just a few days. With advances in robotics, patients can look forward to scar-free surgery.[46] A major expansion in our ability to offer psychological therapies for depression and anxiety will mean that many people who were previously untreated will in future receive treatment based on the best international evidence.

21. Healthcare itself is on a journey where the emphasis of care is shifting to extending wellness and improving health. This is making healthcare more complex, with a broader range of interventions possible. In some areas of practice, such as for acute coronary syndrome, this has led to increased standardisation where the evidence shows that following protocols leads to better outcomes.[47] In others, such as the treatment of paediatric cancers, innovations mean that best practice is constantly changing and evolving.[48] For patients, these medical advances often mean longer and more fulfilling lives. There are, however, broader implications. Greater clinical uncertainty requires both greater professional judgement as to what is the right course of action for an individual patient and a more open and honest discussion of risks to enable patients to make informed decisions.

45 Cornwall is one of the Whole System Demonstrator sites promised on page 120 of the *Our health, our care*, our say White Paper.

46 For more information see Darzi, *Saws and Scalpels to Lasers and Robots – Advances in Surgery* (2007).

47 SA Spinler, "Managing acute coronary syndrome: evidence-based approaches," *Am J Health Syst Pharm*, 2007 Jun 1;64(11 Suppl 7):S14-24.

48 P. Paolucci, "Challenges in prescribing drugs for children with cancer," *Lancet Oncol.*, 2008 Feb;9(2):176-83.

2

## Challenge 6: A changing health workplace

22. In recent years, Britain has become a 'knowledge economy' with the majority of new jobs being in knowledge-based industries.[49] Healthcare has always been a knowledge-led sector, relying on expert learning and depth of experience. Increasing complexity is an integral feature of modern healthcare. With new advances in clinical science and new treatments for patients, come fresh challenges for professionals. Whether in acute or community settings, easy and convenient access to knowledge is an essential part of a modern and effective workplace.

23. Expectations of work in healthcare are changing, with people today seeking *quality work*.[50] Healthcare professionals expect the depth of their expertise to be recognised and rewarded, and their skills to be developed and enhanced. They seek personal fulfilment as well as financial reward.[51] They understand the demands of accountability and welcome transparency as a route to achieving true meritocracy. Staff expect a better work/life balance and more respect and regard for pressures on their time beyond those of their profession.

24. High quality work is not simply a matter of a good deal for staff and for patients. It is also essential to meeting the productivity challenge: high quality workplaces make best use of the talents of their people, ensuring that their skills are up to date, and their efforts never wasted. The public rightly expect their taxes to be put to best use. For those working in the NHS there is a need to reduce unnecessary bureaucracy, freeing up their time to care for patients, within the resources available. Creating high quality workplaces requires great leadership and good management.

## Where we stand today

25. I believe we are well placed to respond to these challenges not only because of the progress made over recent years but also because of the fundamental basis of our NHS as a tax-funded system, based on clinical need rather than ability to pay. In this respect, the NHS is unlike health systems in comparable countries, and is particularly well positioned to respond.

26. For insurance companies, there is no incentive to invest in the prevention of ill health as patients may move to a different scheme. Diagnostics increase the capacity of the NHS to reach out to predict and prevent ill health, but in other systems they increase their capacity to exclude those at risk from the protection they need.

49  Ian Brinkley, *The Knowledge Economy: How Knowledge is Reshaping the Economic Life of Nations*, March 2008, The Work Foundation.

50  For more on the importance of work quality see G. Lowe, *The Quality of Work: A People-Centred Agenda*, 2000.

51  On doctor's motivation see S. Dewar et al., *Understanding Doctors: Harnessing Professionalism*, King's Fund, May 2008.

27. The Wanless Report of 2002 made the case for additional investment in the NHS, to which the Government has responded.[52] The NHS is now funded at close to the EU average.[53] In 2009/10, the NHS budget will exceed £100 billion. The NHS has the financial resources it needs.

28. However, the NHS must use these resources well. Increasing expectations, an ageing population, a rise in lifestyle disease and the cost of new treatments will all impose greater costs.

29. The NHS must respond by improving the quality of care it provides. This is because the evidence shows that, in general, higher quality care works out better for patients and the taxpayer. For instance, day surgery for cataracts delivers the highest quality of care with no admission to hospital.[54] High quality care is safe, meaning no avoidable healthcare associated infections. This is obviously better for patients and also reduces the need for costly post-infection recovery in hospital. Finally, high quality care involves giving the patient more control over their care, including information to make healthy choices, which will reduce their chances of poor health and dependency on the NHS. The answer to the challenges the NHS faces is therefore to focus on improving the quality of care it provides.

52 Wanless, *Securing our Future Health* (2002).
53 In 2008 the UK is expected to spend 9.0% of its GDP on health, compared with an average of 9.5% amongst the 15 pre-enlargement EU members.
54 Cataract extraction was one of a "basket" of 25 procedures recommended by the Audit Commission in 2001 as suitable for day surgery. Day surgery for cataract removal is less than two thirds of the cost of doing it as an inpatient procedure (RCI 2005).

# 3
# High quality care for patients and the public

An NHS that works in partnership to prevent ill health, providing care that is personal, effective and safe

A session at the Tower Hamlets
Exercise and Nutrition Programme,
Mile End Hospital, London

# 3

# High quality care for patients and the public

An NHS that works in partnership to prevent ill health, providing care that is personal, effective and safe

## Introduction

1. This Review is about achieving the highest quality of care for patients and the public. I have heard from patients and staff, and I know from my own experience, that when in the care of the NHS, it is the quality of that care that really matters. People want to know they will receive effective treatment. They want care that is personal to them, and to be shown compassion, dignity and respect by those caring for them. People want to be reassured that they will be safe in the care of the NHS. And whilst most people recognise their health is their responsibility, they also look to the NHS for help.

2. The investment and reform of the past decade have given us the opportunity to pursue this ambitious agenda for patients and the public.

3. Ten years ago, today's quality reform agenda would have seemed particularly challenging. The extra capacity in the NHS today gives all of us the opportunity to focus on improving quality. To achieve that we need to:

   - **Help people to stay healthy**. The NHS needs to work with its national and local partners more effectively, making a stronger contribution to promoting health, and ensuring easier access to prevention services.

   - **Empower patients**. The NHS needs to give patients more rights and control over their own health and care, for more personal care.

   - **Provide the most effective treatments**. Patients need improved access to the treatments they need supported by improved diagnostics to detect disease earlier.

   - **Keep patients as safe as possible**. The NHS must strive to be the safest health system, keeping patients in environments that are clean, and reducing avoidable harm.

## Helping people to stay healthy

4. Our health starts with what we do for ourselves and our families, but the environment we live in influences our decisions and ultimately our health. Some people live in circumstances that make it harder to choose healthy lifestyles. Changing this environment can influence the way people look after their own and their families' health. This is particularly important if we are to tackle inequalities in health status and outcomes.

3

5.  Patients and the public want the NHS to play its part in helping them to stay healthy. Nearly a quarter of people felt health was 'mainly my' responsibility, and a further 60 per cent felt it was 'mainly me with support from the NHS.'[55] Alongside the NHS, we need to ensure that a range of organisations – public and private – play their part in supporting people to stay healthy.

6.  Locally, the NHS and local authorities are working closely together to improve health and wellbeing, prompted by their legal duty to co-operate in improving outcomes for their populations. The duty is based on a formal assessment of people's needs (Joint Strategic Needs Assessments) developed between primary care trusts, local authorities and other local partners, including police authorities and local hospitals, to tackle the most important factors in improving health. These plans focus not only on tackling clear health priorities such as smoking, childhood obesity and teenage pregnancy, but also on broader factors such as poor housing, education, local transport and recreational facilities.

*Focusing on helping prevent ill health*

7.  As well as improving partnership working, the NHS itself has strengthened its contribution to preventing ill health through sustained investment over the past decade. As the visions show, the foundations of good health and healthy lifestyles are laid down in the very earliest stages of life. The Child and Young People's Health Strategy due in the autumn will seek to build on the new Child Health Promotion Programme that sees highly skilled health visitors and school nurses supporting families on health and parenting from pregnancy onwards. It will also bring with it a further focus on improving services for adolescents.[56]

8.  Progress has been made in detecting illnesses earlier and preventing them from worsening, including in cardiac and cancer services. Much of this progress has been achieved through national screening and immunisation programmes. We need to continue this progress.

9.  We will therefore strive to accept and implement every recommendation for screening and vaccination programmes that the relevant national expert committees make.[57] This will be a pledge within the NHS Constitution so that people know these services will be available without question, where they are clinically and cost effective.

55 Primary and Community Care Deliberative Event, run by HCHV, April 2008.

56 *The Children's Plan*, published in December 2007 by the Department for Children, Families and Schools (DCFS) committed to DCFS and the Department of Health publishing a joint child health strategy.

57 These are the Joint Committee on Vaccination and Immunisation (JCVI) and the National Screening Committee (NSC).

10. There remains significant room for improvement, especially across the risk factors identified in chapter two – disease, smoking, excessive drinking, poor diet and lack of exercise. The NHS must now focus on preventing ill health for individuals and giving them the opportunities and support to improve their health.

11. Vascular conditions are major causes of early death, long-term illness and health inequality. These include coronary heart disease, stroke, diabetes and kidney disease. Taken together, they affect over 4.5 million people in England, and are responsible for over 170,000 deaths every year.[58] Some of these deaths could be prevented if people understood their own health status. Where people can act to decrease their chance of developing particular forms of ill health, we want people to understand clearly what the risks are to their health and what they can do to prevent the onset of irreversible disease.

12. Earlier this year we announced help for people to do this through vascular health checks for everyone aged 40-74.[59] These will be introduced from 2009, and rolled out through GPs, pharmacies and community clinics. By 2012, we expect three million people every year to be offered a check, preventing at least 9,500 heart attacks and strokes and 4,000 people from developing diabetes each year. We will make it easy and convenient to access these checks in a variety of places. In particular, we believe that pharmacies have a key role to play as providers of prevention services.[60]

13. We need to raise awareness of this new service. We will do this through a nationwide 'Reduce Your Risk' campaign, which will be launched during 2009 alongside vascular health checks. This campaign will clearly explain what people can do to reduce their risks: stop smoking, maintain a healthy weight, increase physical activity, lower blood pressure. We will also work with third sector groups to reach those less likely to access services.

*Ensuring that people have convenient access to prevention services*

14. Working with their local partners, every primary care trust will commission comprehensive wellbeing and prevention services, with the services offered customised to meet the specific needs of their local populations. This reflects the finding of the SHA staying healthy groups, who called for prevention services on "an industrial scale." Our efforts must be focused on six key goals: tackling obesity, reducing alcohol harm, treating drug addiction, reducing smoking rates, improving

---

58  See Department of Health, *Putting Prevention First*, April 2008.

59  For more information on the rationale for the age range of 40-74 see Department of Health, *Technical consultation on economic modelling of a policy of vascular checks*, June 2008

60  Department of Health, *Pharmacy in England: building on strengths – delivering the future*, April 2008.

3

sexual health and improving mental health. Examples of services that we expect local PCTs to develop and expand include alcohol brief interventions, exercise referral, weight management and talking therapies, and we expect the reach of these services to increase as the NHS seeks to support all of us in making healthier choices.

15. Reflecting this new priority for the NHS, and the need to work together with partners from all sectors of society, we will launch shortly a Coalition for Better Health. The Coalition will be a new set of voluntary agreements between government, private and third sector organisations, focused on the action each needs to take to achieve better health outcomes for the nation. As we announced in *Healthy Weight, Healthy Lives* earlier this year, its initial priority will be combatting obesity by supporting healthier food, more physical activity, and encouraging employers to invest more in the health of their employees.[61]

16. All too often, those living in poverty are poorest in health.[62] As set out in the recent Health Inequalities strategy, the root causes of ill health lie heavily in people's life circumstances.[63] Excellent prevention services are a matter of fairness, and

primary and community services have a pivotal role to play in reaching out to those communities where socio-economic factors are linked to reduced life expectancy and higher prevalence of illness.

17. In my Interim Report, I set out plans to tackle inequalities in primary care by establishing over 100 new GP practices in the areas of the country with the fewest primary care clinicians and the greatest health needs – more often than not, these are our most deprived communities.

18. To improve access to primary care services, my interim report also announced that we would invest additional resources to enable the local NHS to develop over 150 GP-led health centres to supplement existing services. The services provided in these centres will reflect local needs and priorities. Primary care trusts will ensure that these centres are open at more convenient hours that fit with people's lifestyles (8am to 8pm every day) and that they are open to any member of the public, so that people can walk in regardless of which local GP service they are registered with. People will be offered the opportunity to register at these new facilities, should they choose.

19. These health centres will provide additional, convenient access to primary care services, including in the evenings and at weekends. PCTs have been developing proposals locally not only for additional access to GP services, but also to a much

---

61 *Healthy Weight, Healthy Lives*, HM Government, May 2008.

62 See for instance M. Marmot, "The Social Determinants of Health Inequalities," *Lancet* 2005, 365, 1099-1104.

63 Department of Health, *Health Inequalities: Progress and Next Steps*, June 2008.

broader range of services such as diagnostic, mental health, sexual health, social care and healthy living services to match the needs of their communities. This broader range of services will not inhibit any patient's continuity of care. It is precisely because these needs vary that there is no national blueprint.

20. *NHS Next Stage Review: Our Vision for Primary and Community Care* will be published shortly. The main features of that strategy are summarised in this report. NHS primary and community care services are strongly rooted in their local communities and patients, carers and their families rightly value the personal relationships and continuity of care that they provide. The strategy will describe a vision for primary and community care that builds on these strengths and raises our ambitions. It will focus on making services personal and responsive to all, promoting healthy lives and striving to improve the quality of care provided.

21. Currently the incentives for General Practice focus largely on the effective management of long-term conditions rather than seeking to prevent those conditions in the first place. We will change this by supporting family doctors to play a wider role in helping individuals and their families to stay healthy. We will work with professional and patient groups to improve the world-leading Quality and Outcomes Framework to provide better incentives for maintaining

good health as well as good care. Family doctors, practice nurses and other primary and community clinicians will have greater opportunities and incentives to advise people on measures they can take to improve their health. We will support this by investing new resources in the areas that are worst affected by obesity and alcohol-related ill health.

22. For many people, one of the most convenient places to access preventive services is at their place of work. Evidence shows that employers can make a very positive contribution to the health of their employees, and that where they invest in employee health they very often reap benefits in employee motivation, in productivity and in profit too.[64] To encourage this investment, we are working in partnership with the Department for Work and Pensions and Business in the Community to ensure that 75 per cent of FTSE 100 companies report on their employee's health and wellbeing at board level by 2011.

23. Preventing ill health often also means helping people stay in employment. A recent review of the health of the working age population underlined the benefits of work and employment for our

---

64 Wang PS et al., "The costs and benefits of enhanced depression care to employers," *Arch Gen Psychiatry*. 2006 Dec;63(12) found that both employees and employers would benefit if employers improved access to mental health services for their employees.

3

overall health and well-being.[65] It highlighted the rapidly rising risks to long-term health if people are not supported sufficiently early to address issues that stop them from working, with back problems and mental ill health among the most significant. From next year, we will introduce integrated Fit for Work services in primary and community care, bringing together access to musculoskeletal services and psychological therapies for example. This will help people get the support they need to return to appropriate work faster.

## Empowering patients: more rights and control over health and care

24. Over the last decade, the NHS has gradually given patients more control over their own care. People referred for secondary or hospital-based care can now choose freely where they receive their treatment. And increasingly, there is better information available for patients about outcomes of care such as the information at GP-practice level from the Quality and Outcomes Framework.

25. Patients empowered in this way are more likely to take greater responsibility for their own health, and to dedicate their own time, effort and energy to solving their health problems. This partnership is especially important for those with long-term conditions and their

carers. We must therefore continue to empower patients with greater choice, better information, and more control and influence.

### Greater choice

26. Today, people who need to be referred for secondary care have free choice of any hospital or treatment centre – NHS or independent sector – that can provide NHS quality care at the NHS price. Choice gives patients the power they need in the system, as NHS resources follows patients in the choices they make. Where patients find it difficult to express preferences, it is the role of staff to take steps to ensure that patients can benefit from greater choice. Choice in public services is sometimes presented as the pre-occupation of the wealthy and the educated, yet the evidence shows that it is the poorest and least well educated who most desire greater choice.[66] We believe that choice should become a defining feature of the service. A health service without freedom of choice is not personalised. So the right to choice will now be part of the NHS Constitution, ensuring that people become more clearly aware of it.

---

65 Dame Carol Black, *Working for a Healthier Tomorrow*, Crown Copyright, March 2008.

66 The British Social Attitudes survey found that 67% of semi-routine and routine workers want more choice compared to 59% of managerial and professional workers, and 69% of people with no formal educational qualifications want more choice compared to 55% of those with higher educational qualifications. Appleby & Alvarez, *British Social Attitudes Survey 22nd Report, Public Responses to NHS Reform*, 2005.

27. It is because we believe that choice has given more control to patients and helped to develop services that respond to their expectations, that we will now put a stronger focus on extending choice in primary and community care. In 1948, the Government informed members of the public that they had a choice of GP.[67] People can indeed choose which GP practice to register with, but in some areas the degree of choice is still restricted by closed patient lists, by practices saying they are 'open but full', or by narrow practice boundaries. We will support the local NHS, working with GPs, to give the public a greater and more informed choice, not just for GP services but for the wider range of community health services.

28. Providing greater choice of GP will mean developing fairer rewards for practices that provide responsive services and attract more patients. At present, most GP practices receive historic income guarantees that do not necessarily bear relation to the size or needs of the patient population they now serve, or the number of patients they see. We will work with GP representatives to manage the phase out of these protected income payments, so that more resources can go into providing fair payments based on the needs of the local population served by each practice.

## Better information

29. We want patients to make the right choices for themselves and their families. So we will empower them to make *informed* choices. The first step towards this vision was taken with the launch of the NHS Choices website, with a variety of limited quality information (such as Healthcare Commission ratings and MRSA rates at an organisation level).[68] The next stage is to empower patients with clear information on the quality of each service offered by every NHS organisation – across all settings of care.

30. In practice, this means easy-to-understand, service-specific, comparable information available online. The information will be on every aspect of high quality care – on safety such as cleanliness and infection rates, on experiences such as satisfaction, dignity and respect, and on measures of outcomes that include patients' views on the success of treatments. *Chapter 4* sets out in more detail how we will do this. And the NHS Constitution will guarantee that this information on quality will be freely and openly available as well as reliable.

31. In primary care, we will continue to develop the NHS Choices website to include more comparative information about the range of services offered by GP practices, their opening times, the views of local patients, and their performance

---

67 *The New National Health Service*, Central Office of Information for the Ministry of Health, Crown Copyright (1948).

68 NHS Choices can be found at www.nhs.uk

3

against key quality indicators. We will also develop the website so that it offers a simpler way of registering electronically with a GP practice. These national efforts to improve choice of GP should be mirrored at local level, for instance through local NHS information packs for people who have just moved house.

32. During the Review, patients have told us that they need better information and more help to understand how to access the best care, especially urgent care, when they need it. I said in my interim report that we should consider options to introduce a new three-digit telephone number to help people find the right local service to meet their urgent, unplanned care needs. Several of the visions included plans to develop such a number.[69] We will learn from this local work as we consider nationally the costs and benefits of an urgent care number. We will set out further details from this next phase of work later this year.

*Increased control*

33. We have to keep up with the expectations of the public. This will mean allowing people to exercise choice and be partners in decisions about their own care, shaping and directing it with high quality information and support. Empowering patients in this way enables them to use their personal knowledge, time and energy for

solving their own health problems. The fundamental solution to the rise of lifestyle diseases is to change our lifestyles. While the NHS can support and encourage change, ultimately, these are decisions that can only be made by us as individuals. Those with two or more long-term conditions are more likely to be obese, eat less healthily and smoke than those with one or none.[70] People need to know the risks and have the opportunity to take control of their own healthcare. To help with this, the Department of Health will publish a new Patients' Prospectus by the end of this year to provide patients with long-term conditions the information they need about the choices which should be available to them locally and to enable them to self-care in partnership with health and social care professionals.

34. Beyond this, international best practice suggests that control by a patient is best achieved through the agreement of a personal care plan. In Germany, nearly two-thirds of people with long-term conditions have a personal care plan, whereas the same is true for only a fifth of people in this country.[71] Care planning creates packages of care that are personal to the patient. It involves working with professionals who really understand their needs, to agree goals, the services chosen, and how and where to access them. Personal care plans

69 See for instance the NHS East Midlands and NHS London visions.

70 Department of Health, *Long term conditions: Compendium of Information*, January 2008.

71 2006 Commonwealth Fund International Health Policy Survey of Primary Care Physicians.

are agreed by the individual and a lead professional.[72]

35. Over the next two years, every one of the 15 million people with one or more long-term conditions should be offered a personalised care plan, developed, agreed and regularly reviewed with a named lead professional from among the team of staff who help manage their care. The lead professional takes a lead within the care team for advising the patient on how best to access the care that the plan sets out. For people with a serious mental illness, the 'care programme approach' (CPA) has pioneered this approach.[73] Primary care trusts and local authorities have the responsibility to ensure that all this is achieved, as well as offering a choice of treatment setting and provider.

36. Increased control will not be limited to those being cared for, but will also extend to carers. A new strategy has been published, setting out the Government's plans for supporting carers.[74]

37. Achieving the strong partnership that characterises personalised care is only possible through greater 'health literacy'. Too few people have access to information about their care or their own care record.

We will change this. We will expand the educational role of the NHS Choices website. We will introduce HealthSpace online from next year, enabling increasing numbers of patients to securely see and suggest corrections to a summary of their care records, to receive personalised information about staying healthy, and to upload the results of health checks for their clinician(s) to see.[75]

38. All patients will have a right to see the information held about them, including diagnostic tests. We will ensure that patients' right to access their own health records is clear by making this part of the NHS Constitution.

### Greater influence over resources

39. We will increase the influence that patients have over NHS resources. For hospitals, resources already follow the choices that patients make through the Payment by Results system.[76] We will strengthen this by reflecting quality in the payment mechanism and increasing individual control.

40. First, we will make payments to hospitals conditional on the quality of care given to patients as well as the volume. A range of quality measures covering safety (including cleanliness and infection rates), clinical outcomes, patient experience

---

72  This more personalised and joint approach extends the original commitment to care plans in the *Our health, our care, our say* White Paper.

73  Department of Health, *Refocusing the Care Programme Approach*, March 2008.

74  Department of Health, *Carers at the heart of 21st century families and communities*, June 2008.

75  Further details on our plans for information are addressed in the Health Informatics Review, which will be published shortly.

76  In 2008/09, over 60 per cent of the average hospital's income is through Payment by Results.

3

and patient's views about the success of their treatment (known as patient-reported outcome measures or PROMs) will be used.[77]

41. This 'Commissioning for Quality & Innovation' (CQUIN) scheme will encourage all NHS organisations to pay a higher regard to quality. The scheme will build upon best practice found in the NHS and internationally.[78] It will be a simple overlay to the Payment by Results system, forming part of commissioning contracts. Funding will be freed up through reducing the tariff uplift from 2009 to give commissioners dedicated space to pay for improved outcomes. Providers will be rewarded in the first year for submitting data. From no later than 2010, payments will reward outcomes under the scheme. The scheme will be flexible to suit local circumstances. Where PCTs want to go faster, they will be able to apply the principles as soon as they wish. The scheme will be subject to independent evaluation so that it improves as it matures.

42. Second, we will go even further in empowering individual patients. Learning from the experience in both social care and other health systems, and in response to the enthusiasm we have heard from local clinicians, we will explore the

potential of personal budgets, to give individual patients greater control over the services they receive and the providers from which they receive services.[79] Personal health budgets are likely to work for patients with fairly stable and predictable conditions, well placed to make informed choices about their treatment; for example, some of those in receipt of continuing care or with long-term conditions. With a view to national roll out, we will launch a national pilot programme in early 2009, supported by rigorous evaluation. This will enable the NHS and their local authority partners to test out a range of different models.

43. The budget itself may well be held on the patient's behalf, but we will pilot direct payments where this makes most sense for particular patients in certain circumstances. We will legislate to enable these direct payments.

44. The programme will be designed with NHS, local authority, carer and patient group partners, with clear rules. We will ensure that the programme fully supports the principles of the NHS as a comprehensive service, free at the point of use. It will be voluntary – no one will ever be forced to have a budget, and for those that choose to, there will be tailored support

77 Department of Health, *The NHS in England: Operating Framework 2008/9*, December 2007.
78 NHS North West have introduced a scheme to pay for performance.

79 Members of NHS Yorkshire and Humber area's clinical working group on long term conditions advocated exploring personal budgets in healthcare.

to meet their different needs. The programme will be underpinned by safeguards so that no one will ever be denied treatment as a result of having a personal budget, and NHS resources will be put to good use, with appropriate accountability.

*Partnership focused on people*

45. Partnership working between the NHS, local authorities and social care partners will help to improve people's health and wellbeing, by organising services around patients, and not people around services. This will lead to a patient-centred and seamless approach. This is important not only for people regularly using primary, community and social care services, but will also help people's transition from hospitals back in to their homes. It will also reduce unnecessary re-admissions in to hospitals. In addition local NHS organisations should work in partnership with the local authority, 3rd sector and private sector organisations, patients and carers to implement the *Putting People First* transformation programme for social care.[80] This programme sets out the Government's vision for the personalisation of social care. It aims to improve people's health and wellbeing through new mechanisms such as personal budgets.

## Ensuring access to the most effective treatments

46. Patients want the most effective treatments, and staff want to be able to provide them. As the NHS becomes more personal, patients and the public want to be assured that the most clinically and cost effective treatments are available everywhere. During this Review, patients and the public were very clear that they had zero tolerance for variations in access to the most effective treatments. The National Institute for Health and Clinical Excellence (NICE), established in 1999, has developed a worldwide reputation for its work in evaluating health interventions. It has highly regarded, transparent processes for assessing new, licensed drugs and medical technologies to determine clinical and cost effectiveness.

47. It has sometimes taken too long for NICE appraisal guidance to be made available on newly licensed drugs. Guidance has often been published two years or more after a new drug's launch, though NICE has now put in place a faster appraisal process for key new drugs which enables it to issue authoritative guidance on them within a few months of their UK launch. Whilst all primary care trusts have a legal duty to fund drugs that have been positively appraised by NICE, we recognise that patients and the public are concerned that there remains unexplained variation in the way local decisions are made on the funding of new drugs before the appraisal takes place, or where no guidance is issued.

80  *Putting People First, A shared vision and commitment to the transformation of adult social care*, HM Government, December 2007.

3

48. We will take steps to end this so-called 'postcode lottery' for new drugs and treatments. Through the NHS Constitution we will make explicit the right of NHS patients everywhere to positively NICE-appraised drugs and treatments, where their doctor judges that these would be of benefit. The Constitution will also make clear the right of patients to expect rational local decisions on funding of new drugs and treatments. Open and honest explanation will be due if the local NHS decides not to fund a drug or treatment that patient and clinician feel would be appropriate.

49. Furthermore, we will work with NICE to enable them to produce consistently fast guidance on significant new drugs. This will be achieved by making further improvements to the topic selection and appraisal process. It will mean that NICE can issue the majority of its appraisal guidance within a few months of a new drug's launch.

50. In addition, the Secretary of State for Health has recently asked the National Cancer Director, Professor Mike Richards CBE, to review policy relating to patients who choose to pay privately for drugs not funded on the NHS. This specifically targeted review, to report later this year, will make recommendations on whether and how policy or guidance could be clarified or improved.

51. Looking to the future, we will strengthen the horizon scanning process for new medicines in

development. We will involve the industry systematically to support better forward planning and to develop ways of measuring the uptake of clinically and cost effective medicines once introduced. For new clinical technologies, we will simplify the way in which they pass from development into wider use by creating a single evaluation pathway, and will develop ways to benchmark and monitor their successful uptake.

## Keeping patients as safe as possible

52. Continuously improving patient safety should be at the top of the healthcare agenda for the 21st century. The injunction to 'do no harm' is one of the defining principles of the clinical professions, and as my Interim Report made clear, safety must be paramount for the NHS. Public trust in the NHS is conditional on our ability to keep patients safe when they are in our care.

53. In recent years, with additional investment, the NHS has focused on raising levels of cleanliness and reducing rates of healthcare associated infections, including through the measures set out in my Interim Report.[81] Today, rates of MRSA and *C. difficile* are falling – but we must continue to combat healthcare associated infections.[82] For that reason, we have recently announced a tough but fair regime

81  Darzi, *Our NHS, Our Future: Interim Report*, October 2007.
82  For more Information see the DH publication *The Quarter: Quarter 4* 2007-08.

that robustly deals with any failures of safety.[83] Furthermore, the new health and adult social care regulator, the Care Quality Commission (CQC), will be able to use its new enforcement powers in relation to infections from April 2009.[84] This is a full year before the new powers will be available to it in relation to other quality and safety requirements.

54. Infections are only one area where action is needed. Since 2003, we have made great progress on the reporting of safety incidents. The National Reporting and Learning System (NRLS) has received two million reports of adverse incidents ranging from the very minor to the extremely serious. Safety incidents can involve a wide array of factors, from infrastructure, training, treatment protocols, procedure and communication to simple administrative errors. Safety is the responsibility of all staff, clinical and non-clinical.

55. Building on *Safety First*,[85] the next stage is to implement systematic improvement, locally, regionally and nationally. The National Patient Safety Campaign is being launched, led by the service. From April 2009 the NPSA will run an additional, dedicated national patient safety initiative to tackle central line

catheter-related bloodstream infections, drawing lessons from a remarkably successful Michigan initiative on the same topic.[86] The NPSA will run regular patient safety initiatives like this in future.

56. In some parts of the United States, events that are serious and largely preventable such as 'wrong-site' surgery have been designated 'Never Events', and payment withheld when they occur. The NPSA will work with stakeholders in this country to draw up its own list of 'Never Events'. From next year, PCTs will choose priorities from this list in their annual operating plan.

## Conclusion

57. High quality care is care where patients are in control, have effective access to treatment, are safe and where illnesses are not just treated, but prevented. These are manifestations of high quality care – there is much more to be done to place quality right at the heart of the NHS.

83 Department of Health, *Developing the NHS Performance Regime*, June 2008.

84 Subject to the Parliamentary passage of the current Health and Social Care Bill.

85 *Safety First, A report for patients, clinicians and healthcare managers*, Department of Health, December 2006.

86 Hales BM, Pronovost PJ, The checklist – a tool for error management and performance improvement. *J Crit Care* 2006;21(3):231-5 and Berenholtz SM, Pronovost PJ, Lipsett PA, et al. Eliminating catheter-related bloodstream infections in the intensive care unit. *Crit Care Med* 2004;32(10):2014-20.

# 4

# Quality at the heart of everything we do

High quality care throughout the NHS

A patient from Cheltenham and a physiotherapist at the National Spinal Injuries Centre at Stoke Mandeville Hospital, Aylesbury

# 4

# Quality at the heart of everything we do

High quality care throughout the NHS

## Introduction

1.  Having considered what high quality care looks like for patients and the public, we need to think how it becomes integral to the NHS. My Interim Report contained the message that the NHS has an unprecedented opportunity to focus on quality and that this opportunity should be seized.[87] The vision documents show the enthusiasm of frontline clinicians to take up the quality challenge.

2.  If quality is to be at the heart of everything we do, it must be understood from the perspective of patients. Patients pay regard both to clinical outcomes and their experience of the service. They understand that not all treatments are perfect, but they do not accept that the organisation of their care should put them at risk. For these reasons, the Review has found that for the NHS, quality should include the following aspects:[88]

    -   **Patient safety**. The first dimension of quality must be that we do no harm to patients. This means ensuring the environment is safe and clean, reducing avoidable harm such as excessive drug errors or rates of healthcare associated infections.

    -   **Patient experience**. Quality of care includes quality of *caring*. This means how personal care is – the compassion, dignity and respect with which patients are treated. It can only be improved by analysing and understanding patient satisfaction with their own experiences.

    -   **Effectiveness of care**. This means understanding success rates from different treatments for different conditions. Assessing this will include clinical measures such as mortality or survival rates, complication rates and measures of clinical improvement. Just as important is the effectiveness of care from the patient's own perspective which will be measured through patient-reported outcomes measures (PROMs). Examples include improvement in pain-free movement after a joint replacement, or returning to work after treatment for depression. Clinical effectiveness may also extend to people's well-being and ability to live independent lives.

3.  Reforms have improved quality in terms of patient safety and effectiveness of care. For instance, the introduction of standards

87 Darzi, *Our NHS, Our Future: Interim Report*, October 2007.
88 See Darzi, A. *Quality and the NHS Next Stage Review*, Lancet.

4

through National Service Frameworks has led to major progress on tackling illnesses such as cancer and heart disease. Conversations about quality take place in multi-disciplinary teams rather than in corridors. Independent performance assessment and regulation of providers has been introduced. The positive impact of these reforms has been noted by independent commentators such as the Nuffield Trust.[89]

4.  Nevertheless, it is also true that progress has been patchy, particularly on patient experience. The local clinical visions found unacceptable and unexplained variations in the clinical quality of care in every NHS region.[90] They identified important changes that need to be made to raise standards and ensure all services are high quality. The NHS has to keep moving forward to make sure patients benefit from new treatments and technologies.

5.  In my experience, providing high quality care leads to professional pride, and focusing on improving it energises and motivates all NHS staff, clinical and non-clinical alike. I believe we can use that energy and make the achievement of high quality of care an obsession within the NHS. To do this will require seven steps, building

on the cornerstone of existing local clinical governance:

-   **Bring clarity to quality**. This means being clear about what high quality care looks like in all specialties and reflecting this in a coherent approach to the setting of standards.

-   **Measure quality**. In order to work out how to improve we need to measure and understand exactly what we do. The NHS needs a quality measurement framework at every level.

-   **Publish quality performance**. Making data on how well we are doing widely available to staff, patients and the public will help us understand variation and best practice and focus on improvement.

-   **Recognise and reward quality**. The system should recognise and reward improvement in the quality of care and service. This means ensuring that the right incentives are in place to support quality improvement.

-   **Raise standards**. Quality is improved by empowered patients and empowered professionals. There must be a stronger role for clinical leadership and management throughout the NHS.

-   **Safeguard quality**. Patients and the public need to be reassured that the NHS everywhere is providing high quality care. Regulation – of professions and

89 S. Leatherman and K. Sutherland, *The Quest for Quality: Refining the NHS Reforms*, Nuffield Trust, May 2008.

90 See for instance NHS East of England, *Towards the best, together,* May 2008, which notes the huge variation in caesarean section rates between hospitals (from 15% to 27%) and the big variation in consultant level psychology staff across the region.

of services – has a key role to play in ensuring this is the case.

- **Stay ahead**. New treatments are constantly redefining what high quality care looks like. We must support innovation to foster a pioneering NHS.

## Bringing clarity to quality

6.  We will begin by changing the way standards are set, to bring greater clarity to what high quality care looks like. For everyone working in healthcare, keeping up with best practice is a challenging task. The current breadth and depth of guidance is impressive but also daunting. National Service Frameworks have proved effective, but sometimes at the expense of securing improvement more widely across all areas of care and the spectrum of clinical conditions. Many bodies undertake standard setting, and what is desirable versus what is mandatory is often too hard to understand. In addition, NHS staff tell us that the knowledge and information they need to deliver excellent care can be too hard to find.

7.  We will address these problems by transforming the role of NICE, building on its successes and internationally acclaimed reputation. From 2009, it will expand the number and reach of national quality standards, either by selecting the best available standards (including the adoption of the relevant parts of National Service Frameworks) or by filling in gaps. NICE will manage the synthesis and spread of knowledge through NHS Evidence – a new, single

portal, through which anyone will be able to access clinical and non-clinical evidence and best practice, both what high quality care looks like and how to deliver it. Greater clarity on standards, and where to go to find them, will support the commissioning and uptake of the most clinically and cost effective diagnostics, treatments and procedures.

8.  NICE will continue to work openly and collaboratively in partnership at national level and with frontline staff. For frontline clinicians, working with NICE is already considered a valuable opportunity for clinical professional development. In the next stage of its development, I would like to see NICE reach out even more proactively to local clinical communities as well as national ones. A key enabler of this will the establishment of a fellowship programme. I hope that many of the 2,000 frontline clinicians that led this Review locally will apply for fellowship, and that many others will come forward too.

## Measuring quality

9.  The next stage in achieving high quality care, requires us to unlock local innovation and improvement of quality through information – information which shows clinical teams where they most need to improve, and which enables them to track the effect of changes they implement. After all, we can only be sure to improve what we can actually measure.

10. It is important that we have a national quality framework that enables us to publish comparable

4

information on key measures. With the help and support of frontline clinicians, we have begun to identify comparable measures that are currently used by different parts of the service today, and will bring them together into an integrated national set. These national metrics will be developed through discussion with patients, the public and staff. We will announce the first set of quality indicators that will be used nationally by December 2008. And although we will begin with acute services, from next year, we will also develop and pilot a quality framework for community services.

11. The national metrics will be important, but it will be critical that local NHS organisations should sign up to the concept of quality metrics and feel motivated to augment the national indicators with their own measurements of quality. Our aim is for NHS organisations to freely develop the measures that will best help them to review the quality of the services they offer regularly.

12. Within organisations, we know that a defining characteristic of high performing teams is their willingness to measure their performance and use the information to make continuous improvements. We want all clinical teams to follow this best practice and so we will support them by working in partnership with the professional bodies, specialist societies and universities to develop a wider range of useful local metrics, than the national framework. We will also develop 'Clinical Dashboards'

which will present selected national and locally developed measures in a simple graphical format as a tool to inform the daily decisions that drive quality improvement.

13. Dashboards are being piloted by frontline NHS staff in three locations:

- In an East London A&E department, the dashboard presents information, updated every 15 minutes, about how soon patients are seen, assessed and get results from tests, and about patient satisfaction. The dashboard is used by staff and is displayed prominently in the patients' waiting area.

- In Nottingham, a urology surgical team is using the dashboard to present information on length of stay, complications and average operation length.

- In Bolton, a GP practice is working with the local A&E to collect and display information on the number of patients attending A&E and out-of-hours services.

14. Our goal is that every provider of NHS services should systematically measure, analyse and improve quality. They will need to develop their own quality frameworks, combining relevant indicators defined nationally, with those appropriate to local circumstances. This will include quality measures that reflect the visions for improved services that are at the core of this Review.

15. In primary care, the Quality and Outcomes Framework already provides a range of valuable data on quality, particularly for the quality of care for people with long-term conditions. *Chapter 3* set out how we will ensure GP practices will have incentives and opportunities to engage in prevention activity. We will introduce a new strategy for developing the Quality and Outcomes Framework, which will include an independent and transparent process for developing and reviewing indicators. We will discuss with NICE and with stakeholders including patient groups and professional bodies how this new process should work. We will discuss how to reduce the number of organisational or process indicators, and refocus resources on new indicators of prevention and clinical effectiveness. We will explore the scope to give greater flexibility to PCTs to work with primary healthcare teams to select quality indicators (from a national menu) that reflect local health improvement priorities.

## Publishing quality performance

16. Commitments have been made over a number of years to publish information on clinical effectiveness.[91] Too often these commitments have been held up by uncertainties about what was needed to make progress and disagreements about who should be in charge. This is unacceptable. We should be seeking to create a more transparent NHS. It may be a complex task, but we should develop acceptable methodologies and then collect and publish information so that patients and their carers can make better informed choices, clinical teams can benchmark, compare and improve their performance and commissioners and providers can agree priorities for improvement.

17. Therefore, to help make quality information available, we will require, in legislation, healthcare providers working for or on behalf of the NHS to publish their 'Quality Accounts' from April 2010 – just as they publish financial accounts. These will be reports to the public on the quality of services they provide in every service line – looking at safety, experience and outcomes. Easy-to-understand, comparative information will be available on the NHS Choices website at the same time. The Care Quality Commission will provide independent validation of provider and commissioner performance, using indicators of quality agreed nationally with DH, and publish an assessment of comparative performance.

18. The CQC will publish an annual report to Parliament on the provision of NHS care within England. Building on the strengths of the Healthcare Commission and the Commission for Social Care Inspection, the CQC will therefore provide assurance for the public that information about the quality of care is reliable.

---

91 The publication of surgical outcomes was recommended by the then Secretary of State for Health's Response to the Bristol Royal Infirmary Inquiry on 18 July 2001, who acknowledged that this would take time as such data needed to be "robust, rigorous and risk-adjusted."

4

19. I know that patients, staff and the public all want an NHS that is as good as any healthcare system in the world. Meeting this aspiration will require us to understand how we perform compared to other advanced healthcare systems. So we will work with other Organisation for Economic Cooperation & Development (OECD) countries and with the best academic institutions in the world and draw on our new national quality framework to agree some internationally comparable measures.

## Recognising and rewarding quality improvement

20. The NHS should recognise and reward quality improvement. This means putting the right incentives in place to support high quality care.

21. We will ensure that from April 2009 the payment system for providers of NHS services is improved so that it better reflects clinical practice, recognises complexity of care – including the most specialised services – and supports innovation.[92] As outlined in *Chapter 3*, the Commissioning for Quality and Innovation Scheme (CQUIN) will also support local drives for improvement, concentrating on those aspects of quality that most need local attention.

22. We also want organisations that receive NHS funds to be able to plan for long-term improvements

to patient care and ensure best value. For that reason, we will set out projections for tariff uplift and efficiency gains on a multi-year basis, aligning with future Spending Review periods and PCT allocations cycles.

23. Finally, to ensure we apply these principles as widely as possible, we will also extend payment and pricing systems to cover other services. For example, for mental health services, we will develop national currencies available for use from 2010/11. This will allow the comparison and benchmarking of mental health services, supporting good commissioning.

## Raising standards

24. The locally owned nature of this Review has reinforced my belief that change is most effective not only when it responds clearly to patient needs but also when it is driven by clinicians based on their expert knowledge of conditions and care pathways. Change has not always been managed this way in the NHS. We will therefore put a strong clinical voice at every level in the NHS and we will increase our overall capacity to act on standards and information that support quality improvement. Where we have empowered local clinicians, they have risen to the challenge and delivered real improvements for their patients.

25. We will support clinical teams and clinical directors to develop their practice through peer review, continuing professional development and professional

92 For more on the new version of Healthcare Resource Groups (HRG4), which will be used as part of the Payment by Results funding system, please see www.ic.nhs.uk

revalidation. In secondary care, pioneering accreditation schemes have been developed in psychiatric specialties and, with our support, in radiology. The Royal College of General Practitioners is developing an accreditation scheme for GP practices, which is now being piloted and if appropriate, will be adopted nationally by 2010.

26. Locally, primary care trusts, on behalf of the populations that they serve, should challenge providers to achieve high quality care. This will require stronger clinical engagement in commissioning. This must go beyond practice-based commissioning and professional executive committees to involve all clinician groups in strategic planning and service development to drive improvements in health outcomes.

27. This will be achieved through the World Class Commissioning programme, which will hold primary care trusts to account for the involvement of the full range of informed clinicians. The assurance system that has been developed will draw on evidence including a feedback survey from clinicians, the quarterly practice based commissioning survey, practice-based commissioning governance arrangements and the five year strategic plan. This will be supplemented by interviews between the PCT board and a panel of independent experts, one of whom will be a clinician.

28. Senior clinical leadership at a regional level is currently provided by a Regional Director of Public Health, and a Nurse Director in each strategic health authority. By April 2009, the senior clinical leadership within SHAs will be enhanced with the appointment of new, dedicated SHA Medical Directors. Each SHA will bring forward proposals for medical directors that take account of the individual circumstances of the SHA.

29. The SHA medical directors will be responsible for overseeing implementation of the local clinical visions and providing medical leadership to NHS organisations in their area. They will work alongside regional directors of public health and work closely with professional executive committee chairs. They will have professional accountability to the NHS Medical Director at the Department of Health.

30. The senior clinical leadership team within each SHA will be supported by a SHA Clinical Advisory Group, appointed through competition. Each SHA will make proposals on how best to implement these arrangements.

31. The new arrangements will help sustain and support the strong clinical voice exemplified through this Review.

32. We will also ask each SHA to establish a formal Quality Observatory, building on existing analytical arrangements, to enable local benchmarking, development of metrics and identification of opportunities to help frontline staff innovate and improve

4

the services they offer. I expect that each Quality Observatory will wish to make its information available through portals such as NHS Evidence, to be run by NICE, and the NHS Choices website.

33. The Department of Health will continue to have a role in ensuring that the NHS recognises and prepares for national clinical priorities. We will establish a National Quality Board to provide strategic oversight and leadership on quality. It will oversee the work to improve quality metrics, advise the Secretary of State on the priorities for clinical standards set by NICE, and make an annual report to the Secretary of State on the state of quality in England using the internationally agreed comparable measures. The first report will be published by June 2009. It should draw from output of reviews and reports published by the Care Quality Commission and its predecessor on healthcare, the Healthcare Commission.

34. To demonstrate that quality is the responsibility of clinicians and managers throughout the system, the Board will be chaired by the NHS Chief Executive. Membership will include representation from the various national statutory bodies that make up the national 'quality landscape' for health and social care – including professional and statutory bodies. The aim of the Board will be to bring together all those with an interest in improving quality, to align and agree the NHS quality goals, whilst respecting the independent status of participating organisations.

## Safeguarding quality: the role of intelligent regulation

35. Action to underpin this drive for improved quality through tough regulation is already underway. The first step has been to enhance the role of independent regulation, building on the achievements of existing regulators. The new Care Quality Commission will have a stronger focus on compliance and more flexible enforcement powers. It will ensure compliance with registration requirements for safety and wider quality that all health and adult social care providers will be expected to meet in order to be permitted to deliver services. It will provide independent information and assurance that systems for safety and quality are in place and working well, and it will help providers identify areas in need of improvement.

36. We have recently consulted on proposals that the new Care Quality Commission in time should regulate safety and quality for all GP and dental practices.[93] This would mean that, for the first time, any organisation providing primary medical or dental care will be subject to a consistent set of quality standards. The approach must be light-touch, risk-based and proportionate. The CQC will work with patients and the public, the NHS and the professions to develop this approach in practice and to determine where best to deploy its regulatory focus. And in doing so, the CQC will want to take account of the contribution that emerging

93 Department of Health, The future regulation of health and adult social in England, 25 March 2008.

professionally led accreditation schemes can play, both in primary care and elsewhere in health and social care.

## Staying ahead: a pioneering NHS

37. Clinical practice is constantly improving, offering new opportunities to improve the quality of care. This means that if quality is really at the heart of everything we do, accepting, embracing and leading change is an imperative, not an option. Innovation must be central to the NHS. We established the Health Innovation Council to champion innovation for the NHS and help us develop the innovation proposals in this report.

38. We will continue to transform health research in the NHS by implementing, consolidating and building on the Government's strategy, *Best Research for Best Health*, for the benefit of patients and the public. Our researchers have made a great contribution and will continue to do so. However, too often innovation has been defined narrowly, focusing solely on research, when in fact innovation is a broader concept, encompassing clinical practice and service design. Service innovation means people at the frontline finding better ways of caring for patients – improving outcomes, experiences and safety. In this country, we have a proud record of invention, but we lag behind in systematic uptake even of our own inventions.[94]

39. We want best practice everywhere as the platform from which innovation can flourish. This means doing away with outdated practice. Clearer standards from an expanded NICE will support commissioners to secure the best care for patients by disinvesting from superseded treatments, so ensuring NHS resources are focused on the most clinically and cost effective approaches.

40. To support local efforts to address unexplained variation in quality and universalise best practice, we will start to pay prices that reflect the cost of best practice rather than average cost. This will be enabled through the Best Practice Tariffs programme, which we will introduce where the evidence of what is best practice is clear and compelling. We will start in 2010/11 with four high-volume areas where there is significant unexplained variation in practice: cataracts, fractured neck of femur, cholecystectomy, and stroke care. We will discuss this proposal with clinicians and give further information on these areas later this year so that providers can plan in advance of tariff changes. The Best Practice Tariffs programme will be rigorously evaluated, not least to ensure that it is working for all the partners involved in the delivery of care, and if successful, expanded in future years.

41. Innovation will be driven regionally by strategic health authorities who will have a new legal duty to promote innovation. We will support frontline

94 See Darzi, *Healthcare for London: A Framework for Action*, Case for Change reason six, 2007

4

innovation through the creation of a substantial new regional innovation funds held by SHAs. The funds' purpose will be to identify, grow and diffuse innovation. They will be supported and advised nationally, drawing on expertise and experience from those with a track record in fund management to ensure good rates of return on our investment in the future. An independent expert panel will assess local applications and make awards. In addition, we will create new prizes for innovations that directly benefit patients and the public. They will help foster an enterprise and innovation culture within the NHS. The prizes will be designed to engage a wide range of NHS staff and an expert panel and will be focused on tackling some of the major health challenges, such as radical breakthroughs in the prevention and treatment of lifestyle diseases.

42. We want to foster a pioneering health service that makes best use of the talents of NHS staff, the higher education sector and industry. International evidence from continental Europe, North America and the Far East, has demonstrated that patients benefit by bringing together the talents of different sectors. Their skills are harnessed in developing pioneering treatments and service models for patients. We will enable the stronger partnerships that bring these benefits through creating a new opportunity – Health Innovation and Education Clusters.

43. Health Innovation and Education Clusters will bring together many partners, across primary, community and secondary care, universities and colleges, and industry. They will be collaborations that set shared strategic goals for the benefit of member organisations. Their members will run joint innovation programmes that reflect their local needs and distinctiveness. They will also promote learning and education between their members. Bringing NHS organisations and higher education institutions together will enable research findings to be applied more readily to improve patient care.

44. Over time, in keeping with their aspirations and abilities, it will be possible for these clusters to be commissioned to provide postgraduate education and training of all healthcare professionals. This will help ensure that trainees get the breadth, depth and quality of training and teaching to provide the high quality care to which the NHS aspires.

45. Recognising the diversity of expertise and interests, these clusters will not be defined or imposed nationally, but will be enabled to emerge locally. They will build upon and reinforce successful models of collaboration that are already found in the NHS. We will invite applications from December 2008 for assigned status and funding and will award matched funding to proposals that deliver clear benefits to patients, as judged by an expert peer review process.

46. We also intend to foster Academic Health Science Centres (AHSCs) to bring together a small number of health and academic partners to focus on world-class research, teaching and patient care. Their purpose is to take new discoveries and promote their application in the NHS and across the world. Centres such as these will be where breakthroughs are made and then passed directly on to patients on the ward. There is no pre-defined number, although we have heard interest expressed by five to 10 organisations already.

47. The best and most successful AHSCs will have the concentration of expertise and excellence that enables them to compete internationally. For these organisations, the peer set will not be simply this country or our European neighbours. They will compete globally with established centres such as those in the United States, Canada, Singapore, Sweden and the Netherlands.

48. We will define the criteria for becoming an Academic Health Science Centre (AHSC). In recognition of the global dimension, we will establish an international panel of experts to award this status. This will objectively determine whether organisations that aspire to this status have the appropriate concentration of expertise and excellence to be able to compete internationally. Those who have self-designated AHSC status will be subject to review by the international panel of experts.

49. The potential of AHSCs to deliver research excellence and improve patient care and professional education is tremendous. Clear governance arrangements with academe, which ensure this works for both patients and the NHS, will be very important. A number of governance models have already emerged to suit local circumstances; that is preferable to the imposition of a single model. Our approach will therefore be broadly permissive; we are open to proposals for different forms of governance on a case-by-case basis, including, potentially, changing legislation where this would help an AHSC to achieve the optimal governance model to support its success. We will work with interested organisations to develop these over the next year.

**Conclusion**

50. If everyone, from the hospital Chief Executive to the GP receptionist is primarily focussed on achieving high quality care for patients, we will have succeeded. Central initiatives, from fostering innovation to encouraging quality reporting can play their part. However, ultimately if high quality care is to become more than an ideal, we need to free the local NHS to concentrate on quality.

# 5
# Freedom to focus on quality
Putting frontline staff in control

A senior sister from the Neonatal
Intensive Care unit at the Chelsea
and Westminster Hospital, London

# 5

# Freedom to focus on quality

Putting frontline staff in control

## Introduction

1. Our quality agenda can only succeed if the frontline NHS staff are given the freedom to use their talents. I, and my fellow clinicians, come to work to deliver health care. We try to improve our practice, but we need the freedom and opportunity to do so. When given that freedom through the process of this review, 2,000 clinicians, health and social care staff seized the opportunity to define the future of the NHS.

## Unlocking talents

2. Healthcare is delivered by a team. The team includes clinicians,[95] managerial staff and those in supporting roles. All members of the team are valued. The sense of a shared endeavour – that all of us matter and stand together – was crucial in the inception of the NHS.

3. Every member of the team must be pulling in the same direction. Without the surgery receptionist, no patients would have appointments. Without the hospital porter, there would be no patient on the operating table. For patients, the team must go beyond individual organisations – they expect everyone in the NHS (and beyond into other public services such as social care, housing, education and employment) to work together, to give them the high quality, integrated care that they need and want.

4. In the past, the clinician's role within the team has often been confined to a practitioner, an expert in their clinical discipline. Yet frontline staff have the talent to look beyond their individual clinical practice and act as partners and leaders. In future, every clinician has the opportunity to be a:

- *Practitioner*: Clinicians' first and primary duty will always be their clinical practice or service, delivering high quality care to patients based on patients' individual needs. This means working with patients, families and carers in delivering high quality, personal care, the most effective treatments and seeking to keep people healthy as well as treating them when they are sick. It is an agenda that reinforces the importance of professional judgement, creativity and innovation.

95 Clinicians include those staff who provide clinical care to patients and the public, including doctors, dentists, nurses, midwives, healthcare scientists, pharmacists, allied health professionals, clinical support workers and paramedics.

5

- *Partner*: Clinicians must be partners in care delivery with individual and collective accountability for the performance of the health service and for the appropriate use of resources in the delivery of care. Partnership requires clinicians to take responsibility for the appropriate stewardship and management of finite healthcare resources. Partners will be expected to work closely with others in the health service and beyond, such as social care colleagues, children's centres and schools, to manage the balancing of individual and collective needs, integrating care around patients.

- *Leader*: Clinicians are expected to offer leadership and, where they have appropriate skills, take senior leadership and management posts in research, education and service delivery. Formal leadership positions will be at a variety of levels from the clinical team, to service lines, to departments, to organisations and ultimately the whole NHS. It requires a new obligation to step up, work with other leaders, both clinical and managerial, and change the system where it would benefit patients.

5. These three ways in which clinicians can use their talents are already in evidence in parts of the NHS and internationally.[96] The best work on professionalism is also acknowledging clinicians' wider roles in the NHS.[97]

6. The exact balance between practitioner, partner and leader will be different, depending on the professional role undertaken. For those in formal leadership roles, such as clinical directors, a majority of their time is spent as leaders. For many, clinical practice will continue to dominate – though they will still need to work with others as partners and show the necessary leadership to keep practice up-to-date and deliver the best possible care for their patients.

7. What is clear is that this new professionalism, acknowledging clinicians' roles as partners and leaders, gives them the opportunity to focus on improving not just the quality of care they provide as individuals but within their organisation and the whole NHS. We enable clinicians to be partners and leaders alongside manager colleagues through the following principles:

- **Giving greater freedom to the frontline**. We will continue the journey of setting frontline staff, both providers and commissioners, free to use their expertise, creativity and skill to find innovative ways to improve quality of care for patients.

---

96  The formulation "practitioner, partner, leader" builds upon international experience best exemplified by Kaiser Permanente's approach to clinical leadership in the United States.

97  For examples of where this is already taking place, see Doctors in Society (Royal College of Physicians 2005) and *Understanding Doctors: Harnessing Professionalism* (King's Fund and Royal College of Physicians 2008).

- **Creating a new accountability**. Setting NHS staff free from central control requires a new, stronger accountability that is rooted in the people that the NHS is there to serve. It means the service should look out to patients and the communities they serve not up the line.

- **Empowering staff**. Professionals need to be empowered to make the daily decisions that improve quality of care and we will enable this to happen.

- **Fostering leadership for quality**. All these steps together create the right environment for high quality care to happen, but we need to further develop clinical and managerial leadership.

## Giving greater freedom to the frontline

*Acute, mental health, and ambulance trusts*

8.  The journey of setting NHS organisations free from central direction began with the creation of NHS trusts and, subsequently, NHS foundation trusts. It continues. Our commitment to making acute, mental health and ambulance trusts into NHS foundation trusts remains strong. It is our clear ambition that in future hospital care will be provided by NHS foundation trusts. In order to achieve this, we will aim to accelerate the rate at which existing NHS trusts achieve NHS foundation trust status.

9.  We will extend these freedoms to community providers, exploring a range of options including social enterprises and community foundation trusts. However, there are some providers, for example high secure units, where NHS foundation trust status is not appropriate. Here we will aim to give similar freedoms to organisations, which achieve and maintain similar levels of good governance and financial stability to those required of NHS foundation trusts.

10. It is important that provider organisations enjoy these new and existing freedoms in the context of the national framework. We will therefore continue to ensure that FTs and other providers meet agreed standards for quality of care and choice, and take account of the new NHS Constitution.

11. The freedom of NHS foundation trusts to innovate and invest in improved care for patients is valuable and essential. We welcome recent initiatives that have seen some NHS foundation trusts share the proceeds of their success with all of their staff, from the porter to the senior clinician, and encourage more to do likewise.[98] These autonomous organisations are ideally placed to respond to patient expectations of high quality care.

---

98  Gloucestershire Hospitals NHS foundation trust announced that all staff would benefit from a £100 bonus, BBC Online, 14 December 2007.

5

## Community services

12. We now need to give greater freedom to those working in community services. So far, they have not had the same opportunities for more autonomy. Over a quarter of a million nurses, midwives, health visitors, allied health professionals, pharmacists and others work in community health services. They have a crucial role to play in providing some of the most personalised care, particularly for children and families, for older people and those with complex care needs, and in promoting health and reducing health inequalities.

13. We believe that staff working in community services deserve the same deal as those working in any other part of the NHS. They speak with passion about the potential for using their professional skills to transform services, but are frustrated at the historic lack of NHS focus on how to free up these talents. We will support the development of vibrant, successful provider services that systematically review quality and productivity, including new ways of working in partnership with others, to free up more time for patient care and to improve health outcomes.

14. We will support the NHS in making local decisions on the best governance and organisational models to support the development of flexible, responsive community services. Some primary care trusts have already done this by developing arm's-length provider organisations that remain accountable to the Board. In other areas, the NHS is exploring new approaches such as community NHS foundation trusts or social enterprises.

15. We recognise concerns about staff pension rights when new organisational arrangements are being introduced. Where PCTs and staff choose to set up social enterprise organisations, transferred staff can continue to benefit from the NHS Pension Scheme, while they work wholly on NHS funded work. We will support local decision-making by drawing together and publishing advice on this range of organisational options and their implications for issues such as governance, patient choice, competition and employment.

16. We will also encourage and enable staff to set up social enterprises by introducing a staff 'right to request' to set up social enterprises to deliver services. PCTs will be obliged to consider such requests, and if the PCT board approves the business case, support the development of the social enterprise and award it a contract to provide services for an initial period of up to three years.

## NHS commissioners

17. NHS commissioners, working with their local authority partners through mechanisms such as joint strategic needs assessments, exist to champion the interests of patients, families and the communities in which they live to get the right care, in the right place,

at the right time. They manage the local health system on behalf of patients, the public and staff. The work that Sir Ian Carruthers OBE has led during this Review has shown how commissioners can exercise their responsibility to secure high quality sustainable care for their populations including in rural areas through a range of innovative delivery models. The World Class Commissioning programme is designed to raise ambitions for a new form of commissioning that deliver better health and well-being for the population, improving health outcomes and reducing health inequalities – adding life to years and years to life.[99]

18. This programme has tremendous potential and needs to be challenging about the capability of many of our commissioners and how far we have got with practice-based commissioning. It must provide strong support and encouragement to PCTs to develop quickly. As part of this programme, where primary care trusts have demonstrated that they are improving health outcomes, they will be given greater freedom over the priorities they set and the methods, people and approaches they employ. We will set out these freedoms in the autumn.

19. PCTs are the leaders of the local NHS, and should be seen this way. All PCTs will be free to take the name of their locality, so that instead of being 'somewhere PCT', they are 'NHS somewhere', e.g. NHS Blackpool. This properly reflects that they are the NHS organisation responsible and accountable for the health of the population of that area.

20. We will support primary care trusts as they become World Class Commissioners, with both local and national development resources. As part of this, the Department of Health, on behalf of the strategic health authorities, will establish a list of independent sector organisations that can help primary care trusts to develop the capabilities of their management boards.

## Creating a new accountability

21. With greater freedom must come a new and enhanced accountability. As the NHS achieves once aspirational targets such as 18 weeks from referral to treatment, halved infections rates, and a maximum wait of four hours in accident and emergency, so these ambitions become established as minimum standards. In future, new and essential national challenges will be met through robust minimum standards and by ensuring that national priorities are reflected in local commissioning. There will be no additional top-down targets beyond the minimum standards.

22. Our new approach to accountability will be through openness on the quality of outcomes achieved for

99  For more on world class commissioning see Department of Health, *World Class Commissioning: Competencies and Vision*, December 2007.

5

patients. Professional regulation has ensured that practitioners are accountable to their individual patients during their episode of care. By focusing on the overall outcome, it means that the new accountability is for the whole patient pathway – so clinicians must be partners as well as practitioners. All the different parts of the system – different organisations and professional groups – must stack up behind one another to achieve the best outcome for patients.

23. There will be no national targets set for quality performance, but, as explained in Chapter 4, the outcomes achieved by every NHS organisation will be openly available. In this way, clinicians, and the organisations they work in, will be held to account by their patients, their peers and the public. Measuring and valuing what matters most to patients, the public and staff is the way in which we will enable the NHS to make progress towards high quality care. We believe this transparency will facilitate meaningful conversations between teams and members of teams about how they can continuously improve the quality of care they deliver.

24. This transparency must not be limited to acute health services. Therefore, from next year, we will develop and pilot a quality framework for community services. Later this year, we will complete work on a standard, but flexible, contract to enable commissioners to hold community health services to account for quality and health improvement. We will also increase transparency by moving away from 'block contract' funding.

25. NHS commissioners will be held to account for the quality of health outcomes that they achieve for the populations they serve, including the most vulnerable or excluded people with complex care needs. We have developed a new assurance system that combines local flexibility with strengthened accountability.[100] It is one nationally consistent approach, managed locally by strategic health authorities, and includes an annual assessment of health outcomes, competences and governance as well as providing a commentary on their potential for improvement. All primary care trusts will have implemented the assurance system by March 2009, and the first results will be formally published in March 2010.

## Empowering staff

26. If clinicians are to be held to account for the quality outcomes of the care that they deliver, then they can reasonably expect that they will have the powers to affect those outcomes. This means they must be empowered to set the direction for the services they deliver, to make decisions on resources, and to make decisions on people.

27. In acute care, giving nurse managers authority and control over resources will lead to better, safer, cleaner wards and a higher quality patient experience. Giving clinical directors the power to make decisions on the services they offer, the appraisal and management of their staff and the

100 Department of Health, *World Class Commissioning Assurance System*, June 2008.

way in which they spend their budgets will lead to better quality outcomes for patients.[101] Through our new approach to 'leadership for quality' we will support clinicians as they take on these roles.

28. The purpose of practice-based commissioning is to empower family doctors and community clinicians to assemble high quality care around the needs of patients. It should put clinical engagement at the heart of the commissioning process. We have heard the message, however, that it has not lived up to this aspiration. That is why we will work with the NHS and with the professions to redefine and reinvigorate it.

29. We will give stronger support to practice-based commissioning. This means we will provide incentives for a broader range of clinicians to get involved, so that it brings family doctors together with other community clinicians and with specialists working in hospitals to develop more integrated care for patients. We will distinguish more clearly between the collaborative, multi-professional work involved in commissioning better care for GP practice populations and the role of GP practices in providing an enhanced range of services for their patients. And we will ensure that primary care trusts are held fully to account for the quality of their support for practice based

commissioning, including the management support given to PBC groups and the quality and timeliness of data (e.g. on budgets, referrals and hospital activity).

30. We will empower clinicians further to provide more integrated services for patients by piloting new integrated care organisations (ICOs) bringing together health and social care professionals from a range of organisations – community services, hospitals, local authorities and others, depending on local needs. The aim of these ICOs will be to achieve more personal, responsive care and better health outcomes for a local population (based on the registered patient lists for groups of GP practices). We will invite proposals shortly.

## Fostering leadership for quality

31. Greater freedom, enhanced accountability and empowering staff are necessary but not sufficient in the pursuit of high quality care. Making change actually happen takes leadership. It is central to our expectations of the healthcare professionals of tomorrow. There are many routes to excellent leadership and we do not claim to have all the answers. But we do want people to be able to have meaningful conversations that transcend organisational boundaries. That is why we have identified the core elements of any approach to leadership, which we expect all those leading change in the NHS to be clear about:

101 Evidence from the US shows that hospitals with a higher proportion of clinically trained managers are better managed (Source: McKinsey analysis).

5

- **Vision**. What quality improvements they are trying to achieve and how it will benefit patients and local communities.

- **Method**. How they will make change happen – the management method they will use for implementation, continuous improvement and measuring success.

- **Expectations**. What the difference will mean for people, the behavioural change that will be necessary and the values that underpin it.

32. As explained in the publication *Leading Local Change*,[102] change in the NHS should always be of benefit to individual patients and the population as a whole, should be clinically driven and locally led, with patients, the public and staff involved. In the NHS constitution, we pledge to staff that they will be engaged in the decisions that affect them. Leadership has been the neglected element of the reforms of recent years. That must now change.

33. It is unrealistic to expect NHS staff to take on leadership without action to make it integral to training and development. So we will explore ways to ensure that the undergraduate curricula for all medical and nursing students reflect the skills and demands of leadership and working in the NHS. We will also ensure that leadership development

is an integral part of modernising careers programmes for other healthcare professions.

34. For those at a postgraduate or equivalent stage in their careers, we will explore ways to ensure that both the curricula and appraisal processes reflect the importance of learning leadership skills. For those with a particular interest in leadership, we will support strategic health authorities and health innovation & education clusters to establish Clinical Leadership Fellowships so that they have dedicated time to spend on enhancing their leadership skills.

35. The local NHS already makes considerable investments in leadership development programmes, for clinicians and managers alike. We have heard that these can be variable in their scope and standard. That is why we will introduce a new standard in healthcare leadership, the Leadership for Quality Certificate. It will operate at three levels. Level 1 will be for members of clinical and non-clinical teams with an interest in becoming future leaders. Level 2 will be for leaders of team and service lines, and Level 3 will be for senior directors (e.g. medical, nursing, operations).

36. At the most senior levels, we will identify and support the top 250 leaders in the NHS. This group will include both clinical and non-clinical leaders. They will get close support in their personal development, mentoring, and active career management.

102 Darzi A., *NHS Next Stage Review: Leading Local Change* (2008).

37. We will establish an NHS Leadership Council which will be a system-wide body chaired by the NHS Chief Executive, responsible for overseeing all matters of leadership across healthcare, including the 250 leaders. It will have a particular focus on standards (including overseeing the new certification, the development of the right curricula, and assurance) and with a dedicated budget, will be able to commission development programmes.

38. The NHS Medical Director and National Clinical Directors will also work with senior clinicians to ensure that clinical leadership becomes a stronger force within the NHS. Compared to healthcare organisations in the US, such as Kaiser Permanente, the NHS has very few clinicians in formal leadership roles. For senior doctors, the operation of the current Clinical Excellence Awards Scheme will be strengthened – to reinforce proposals in this chapter to drive quality improvement. New awards, and the renewal of existing awards, will become more conditional on clinical activity and quality indicators; and the Scheme will encourage and support clinical leadership. The scheme will also become more transparent, with applications being publicly available. The profession will be involved in developing and introducing these amendments. In making national awards, the independent Advisory Committee on Clinical Excellence Awards (ACCEA) will have regard to advice from the National Quality Board and the NHS Leadership Council.

39. Finally, leadership is not just about individuals, but teams. Successful organisations are led by successful Boards. We will immediately commission a new development programme for trust boards through the NHS Chief Executive and the new NHS Leadership Council. In addition, we will encourage the development of Masters-level programmes which are relevant to the health sector by providing matched funding to SHA-commissioned programmes.

## Conclusion

40. NHS staff make the difference for patients and communities. It is through unlocking talent that we will achieve high quality care across the board. Many of the features described in this chapter already exist in the best of the NHS, but not systematically so.

41. We seek to change that not by central control, but by freeing NHS staff and organisations to make the right decisions. Therefore, we will extend and improve existing reforms such as NHS foundation trusts and practice based commissioning. Through these changes, healthcare professionals will be not just practitioners, but partners and leaders.

# 6

# High quality work in the NHS

Supporting NHS staff to deliver high quality care

Nursing sister and her young patient at Brune Medical Centre Gosport, Hampshire

# 6

# High quality work in the NHS

Supporting NHS staff to deliver high quality care

1.  To encourage staff who commission and provide NHS services to take up new opportunities and freedom, we must ensure they can benefit from supportive working environments. High quality work means well-designed, worthwhile jobs, support for learning and development, in high quality workplaces, with NHS staff being respected for the caring and compassionate nature of the services they provide.

2.  There has been significant change over the past decade. Pay and conditions have been made fairer. This was an almost silent revolution in making sure that the NHS recognises and rewards the talents of all its staff. Significant workforce contracts were changed, in partnership with the professions. There was an unprecedented investment in education and training that saw the largest expansion in the numbers of doctors, nurses, and other clinicians for a generation.

3.  The service is no longer a single national employer – staff involved in NHS services are employed by their respective organisations, and the first steps to improving the quality of work must always be taken locally. Nevertheless, there are two issues that we face nationally and require national solutions:

*   **High quality workplaces**. We will be clear about what we expect of one another, what staff can expect of NHS employers, and take practical steps to improve the quality of workplaces.

*   **High quality education and training**. Working in partnership with professional representatives, we have developed proposals to improve the system of workforce planning, commissioning and the provision of education and training. The key features are described here, with the technical details in a separate document *NHS Next Stage Review: A High Quality Workforce* published alongside this report. Education and training also extends to ensuring that NHS managers have the skills they require.

## High quality workplaces

4.  I know from experience that working in the NHS can sometimes be frustrating, and I have heard that message over the course of the Review. The great strength of the NHS is that we are all part of the same system. This should mean that we are all able to work effectively together for the benefit of patients. Too often, however, when NHS work cuts across organisations the needs

6

of patients are not put first. There is a tendency to put the perceived interest of the organisations first, and to shirk responsibility for patients. There also remains an infuriating 'not invented here' resistance to adopting new ways of working that can improve patient care.

5. That is why we need to be clear about what it is that we stand for and what we expect of one another. NHS-wide values transcend individual organisations. They are a great strength but we do not often talk explicitly about them. Over the past year, we have carried out extensive work to identify and understand the values of patients, the public and NHS staff. These values are what patients, staff and the public tell us they stand for. They are included in the draft NHS Constitution.

The NHS values have been derived from extensive discussions with staff, patients and the public. They are:

- **Respect and dignity**. We value each person as an individual, respect their aspirations and commitments in life, and seek to understand their priorities, needs, abilities and limits. We take what others have to say seriously. We are honest about our point of view and what we can and cannot do.

- **Commitment to quality of care**. We earn the trust placed in us by insisting on quality and striving to get the basics right every time: safety, confidentiality, professional and managerial integrity, accountability, dependable service and good communication. We welcome feedback, learn from our mistakes and build on our successes.

- **Compassion**. We find the time to listen and talk when it is needed, make the effort to understand, and get on and do the small things that mean so much – not because we are asked to but because we care.

- **Improving lives**. We strive to improve health and wellbeing and people's experiences of the NHS. We value excellence and professionalism wherever we find it – in the everyday things that make people's lives better as much as in clinical practice, service improvements and innovation.

- **Working together for patients**. We put patients first in everything we do, by reaching out to staff, patients, carers, families, communities, and professionals outside the NHS. We put the needs of patients and communities before organisational boundaries.

- **Everyone counts**. We use our resources for the benefit of the whole community, and make sure nobody is excluded or left behind. We accept that some people need more help, that difficult decisions have to be taken – and that when we waste resources we waste others' opportunities. We recognise that we all have a part to play in making ourselves and our communities healthier.

6. These values are the best of the NHS and should inform and shape all that we do. The NHS-wide values are not exclusive – they can and should sit side-by-side with the particular values in any individual organisation, supporting and reinforcing one another. But they should guide our behaviour when working *across* organisations in the system. Living up to their letter and spirit should lead to higher quality workplaces and better services for those who use the NHS.

7. We believe that being clear about our values should help ensure high quality work. But staff are rightly keen to know the practical differences we will make too. In the NHS Constitution we will therefore make four pledges to all NHS staff, from the porter to the community nurse, the medical director to the chief executive. The NHS will strive to:

   • Provide all staff with well-designed, rewarding jobs that make a difference to patients, their families and carers, and communities.

   • Provide all staff with personal development, access to appropriate training for their jobs, and line management support to succeed.

   • Provide support and opportunities for staff to keep themselves healthy and safe.

   • Actively engage all staff in decisions that affect them and the services they provide, individually and through representatives. All

staff will be empowered to put forward ways to deliver better and safer services for patients and their families.

8. Just as the quality of care needs to be measured and published, the same approach should apply to the quality of work. That is why we have agreed with the Healthcare Commission that staff satisfaction will be an indicator in the annual evaluation of NHS trusts and NHS foundation trusts.

9. We will empower staff to hold their employers to account for the investment they make in learning and development. We will require every organisation that receives central funding for education and training to adopt the Government Skills Pledge,[103] to nominate a member of the board to be responsible, and to publish its annual expenditure on continuing professional development so that present and future employees can make choices that are more informed.

10. We will support staff with easier access to the tools they need to do their jobs. We will establish mystaffspace as a convenient, one-stop portal for all staff. Through it they will be able to access the new NHS Evidence knowledge portal and get information on what high quality care looks like and how to deliver it, tailored to their own professional expertise and interests. They will also be able to access information on

---

103 http://inourhands.lsc.gov.uk/
employersSkillsPledge.html

6

performance against the NHS quality framework, their own personal staff records, their credentials, and a log of their learning and development. NHS Mail will be there too. Mystaffspace will give all NHS professionals better access to the information they need to deliver excellent patient care.

## High quality education and training

11. High quality care for patients is an aspiration that is only possible with high quality education and training for all staff involved in NHS services. They provide care in a changing healthcare environment. New roles are emerging. New technology is changing the way they work. Patients and the public, quite rightly, have increasing expectations of personalised care. Workforce planning, education and training needs to change to enable staff to respond more effectively and flexibly to this dynamic environment.

12. The focus needs to be on the roles, education and training and careers paths that will enable the NHS to deliver their visions for quality care. We have worked in partnership with all the professions and the service and many others to identify the changes that are needed to map out a bright future. The issues highlighted here are addressed comprehensively in the *NHS Next Stage Review: A High Quality Workforce* published today alongside this report.

*Clearer roles*

13. For all health professions, we are working in partnership with their professional bodies, employers and other stakeholders to define the unique role and contribution of each of them and how their roles are changing across the pathways of care. From this starting point, and with excellent quality of care as our primary, unifying goal, we will work together to define the skills and expertise they require, and ensure that these are underpinned by appropriate educational standards and programmes.

14. We will demonstrate how these roles link with one another by establishing explicit career pathways, which make career progression clearer, easier and more flexible. We will also introduce modularised, accredited training packages and strengthen educational governance to ensure that all clinical staff have the opportunity to develop their skills throughout their careers for the benefit of patients, employers and their own career progression.

15. We will also continue our work to modernise clinical careers so that jobs and career opportunities continuously improve.

16. Foundation periods of preceptorship for nurses at the start of their careers help them begin the journey from novice to expert. There will be a threefold increase in investment in nurse and midwife preceptorships. These offer protected time for newly qualified nurses and midwives to learn from their more senior colleagues during their first year.

## A locally led approach

17. Our approach to reforming workforce planning and education mirrors that for the provision of high quality care – a belief that quality is best achieved by devolving decision making to the frontline in an environment of transparency and clear accountabilities and where the role of education commissioner and education provider are clearly separated. We will ensure that the workforce is able to meet the needs of patients by developing workforce elements of service plans, using the eight pathways of care of the Review as the basis for identifying what patients need, now and in the future.

18. The new system will require leadership and management of workforce planning and education commissioning throughout the NHS. This approach requires a stronger and more constructive partnership with all professions. That is why we are establishing new professional advisory bodies to enable the professions to contribute to strategic workforce development at all levels. They will bring a single coherent professional voice to advise on how best to achieve our vision of the high quality education and training that underpins high quality care for patients.

19. We will establish an independent advisory non-departmental public body, Medical Education England (MEE), by the end of this year, to advise the Department of Health on the education and training of doctors, dentists, pharmacists and healthcare scientists which needs to be planned nationally. MEE nationally will be supported by similar advisory bodies in every NHS region. Together, they will provide scrutiny and advice on workforce plans and education commissioning strategies to ensure that the NHS has the right quantity and quality of doctors, dentists, pharmacists and healthcare scientists for the future. We will work with the other professions to decide what other national advisory boards are required, recognising the contribution of the diversity of professional roles within multi-disciplinary team to deliver effective evidence-based care.

20. The national and local professional advisory bodies and the wider healthcare system will be supported by a Centre of Excellence, which, from April 2009, will provide objective long-term horizon scanning, capability and capacity development for workforce planning functions, and the development of technical planning assumptions. It will also enable capacity and capability to make the system work.

## Fair and transparent funding

21. We are reforming the funding of education and training to make it fairer, more transparent and ensure that it is used for the purpose for which it is intended. It is for those reasons that we will replace the current historical funding arrangements for the Medical

6

Professional Education and Training (MPET) budget with a tariff based system where the funding follows the trainee. These arrangements will reward quality, promote transparency and protect investment in education and training. With clarity about the resources dedicated to education and training, education commissioners will be empowered to hold providers of that education and training to account, also taking into account the 'voice' and choices of trainees.

22. Nationally, we will seek to extend apprenticeship opportunities in the service – recognising that healthcare support staff – clinical and non-clinical – are the backbone of the service. We will therefore double our investment in apprenticeships over the next four years, and continue to work with trade unions and Skills for Health to identify the appropriate use of apprenticeships within each clinical career framework, and in non-clinical roles.

23. 60 per cent of staff who will deliver NHS services in 10 years time are already working in healthcare. We need to make sure that they are able to keep their skills and knowledge up to date so that they can provide services that meet the changing needs of both patients and local communities. Continuing professional development (CPD) is rightly the responsibility of individual employers. Some do this well, but

this is not always the case[104]. We therefore intend to strengthen the arrangements to ensure staff have consistent and equitable opportunities to update and develop their skills.

24. These and other changes set out in *NHS Next Stage Review: A High Quality Workforce* will ensure that we have a system for workforce planning, education and training that will be sustainable for the long term. Staff will have clearer career frameworks and be able to make informed careers choices. Employers will have a stronger voice in workforce planning and education commissioning and provision and a more flexible workforce. Patients will receive high quality care delivered by highly trained staff and planned around their needs. The public will receive better value for money from national education resources.

*Support for managers*

25. NHS management includes both those who have clinical backgrounds and those who do not. Regardless of whether they have a clinical or non-clinical background, managers and frontline clinicians must forge a strong partnership, sharing successes or setbacks. In all cases, managers must be involved in the core business of clinical practice, helping, supporting and challenging clinicians to deliver the best possible care for

104 Although standard, consistent information on training is very difficult to obtain due to the variety of approaches organisations take in budgeting for training.

patients. This means ensuring that systems work effectively, whether they be patient flows, community disease management, theatre operations or commissioning services.

26. Support already exists to help managers develop these skills. Indeed, the existing programmes for management development are often applauded. These include the award-winning Management Trainee Scheme (MTS) for graduates, the Gateway scheme for individuals from sectors other than health, and the Breaking Through scheme that supports black and minority ethnic people that wish to pursue careers in NHS management. Although the MTS welcomes applications from qualified clinicians who wish to become full-time managers, at present there is no dedicated scheme for clinicians wishing to develop their management and leadership skills.

27. Therefore, we will establish a new programme to equip and support clinicians in leadership and management roles. It will be called the 'Clinical Management for Quality' programme. It will be dedicated to those clinicians leading clinical services lines, with a particular focus on clinical directors and leaders in primary care who are running practice-based commissioning or integrated care organisations.

28. As responsibility is devolved to the local NHS, there will be greater scrutiny of managers. Whilst the overwhelming majority of NHS

managers meet high professional standards every day, a very small number of senior leaders sometimes demonstrate performance or conduct that lets down their staff, their organisations and the patients that they serve. We do not believe a full-blown system of statutory professional regulation – akin to a General Medical Council – would be proportionate at this time, but the Department will work with the profession, the NHS and other stakeholders to ensure that there are fair and effective arrangements to prevent poorly performing leaders from moving on to other NHS organisations inappropriately. While an enhanced Code of Conduct for managers will underpin this, we will consider whether more effective recruitment procedures or a more formal system of assuring suitability for future employment would provide more effective and proportionate safeguards.

## 29. Conclusion

30. Just as patients deserve high quality care, so NHS staff deserve high quality work. If frontline staff are going to focus on improving the quality of care provided by the NHS, they need the right working environments and the right training and education.

# 7

# The first NHS Constitution

Secured today for future generations

# 7

# The first NHS Constitution
Secured today for future generations

1. The NHS belongs to the people. It is there to improve our health, supporting us to keep mentally and physically well, to get better when we are ill and, when we cannot fully recover, to stay as well as we can. It works at the limits of science – bringing the highest levels of human knowledge and skill to save lives and improve health. It touches our lives at times of basic human need, when care and compassion are what matter most.

2. To provide high quality care for all, the NHS must continue to change. But the fundamental purpose, principles and values of the NHS can and must remain constant. Setting this out clearly, along with the rights and responsibilities of patients, the public and staff, will give us all greater confidence to meet the challenges of the future on the basis of a shared understanding and common purpose.

3. That is why in my interim report I committed to exploring the merits of introducing a Constitution for the NHS. As a result of the work of this Review, I am now convinced that there is a strong case for introducing the first NHS Constitution.

**The case for a constitution**

4. An NHS Constitution will:

- **Secure the NHS for the future**. The Constitution will set out clearly the enduring principles and values of the NHS, and the rights and responsibilities for patients, public and staff.

- **Empower all patients and the public**. Patients already have considerable legal rights in relation to the NHS, but these are scattered across different legal instruments and policies. Some are obscure; many people are not aware of all of their existing rights. The Constitution will empower all patients by summarising all existing rights in one place.

- **Empower and value staff**. NHS services are provided by over 1.3 million staff. Those staff are our most important resource. For the NHS Constitution to be an enduring settlement, it needs to reflect what we are offering to staff: our commitment to provide all staff with high quality jobs along with the training and support they need.

7

- **Create a shared purpose, values and principles**. As the NHS evolves, a wider range of providers, including those from the third and independent sectors are offering NHS-commissioned services. Patients expect that wherever they receive their NHS-funded treatment, the same values and principles should apply. All organisations are part of an integrated system for the benefit of patients. That is why we will set out the purpose, principles and values for the NHS in the Constitution. We propose that all organisations providing NHS services are obliged by law to take account of the Constitution in their decisions and actions.

- **Strengthen accountability through national standards for patients and local freedoms to deliver**. The NHS is held to account nationally through Parliament, even though services are delivered locally. The Constitution is an opportunity to clarify and strengthen both national and local accountability. In discussions with patients, public and staff, we have received a clear message that they are committed to the NHS as a national system, paid for out of general taxation; from which they can expect certain standards of care and access. The draft NHS Constitution therefore makes clear what people can expect from the NHS no matter where they live.

## How the Constitution was developed

5.  The NHS Constitution that we are publishing in draft today has been developed in partnership with patients, public, staff and a number of experts.

6.  During this extensive programme of development, engagement and research we heard that:[105]

    - To qualify as a Constitution, the document needed to be short and enduring

    - The Constitution should be flexible and not hold the NHS back in terms of its ambitions for improving the quality of care

    - For the Constitution to be meaningful it must have bite, with means for enforcement and redress, not just warm words or aspirations

    - There was no appetite for a 'lawyers' charter', and concern that we should avoid fuelling litigation

## Our first NHS Constitution

7.  The draft NHS Constitution now sets out in one place the purpose, principles and values of the NHS, and the rights and responsibilities of patients, the public and NHS staff.

---

105 This included a literature review conducted by the London School of Hygiene and Tropical Medicine looking at international experience; Elizabeth Clery, *Trends in Attitudes to Health Care 1983 to 2005: Report based on results from the British Social attitudes Survey*; a series of discussion events with patients, the public and staff; and meetings with leading experts.

8. It reaffirms the commitment to a service which is for everyone, based on clinical need and not an individual's ability to pay.

9. As well as collecting together important rights for both patients and staff, it sets out a number of pledges which reflect where the NHS should go further than the legal minimum. Each right or pledge is backed up by an explanation, in the accompanying *Handbook to the NHS Constitution*, on how they will be enforced and where to seek redress.

10. We intend to legislate, as soon as Parliamentary time allows, to require:

- All NHS bodies and private and third sector providers providing NHS services to take account of the Constitution in their decisions and actions

- Government to renew the NHS Constitution every 10 years, with the involvement of the patients who use it, the public who fund it and the staff who work in it

11. The *Handbook to the NHS Constitution* will be refreshed at least every three years. As well as setting out the legal basis for all of the rights, it sets out how the performance management and regulatory regime of the NHS will ensure that the pledges in the Constitution are delivered.

## Accountability in the NHS

12. The NHS remains a national health service, funded through national taxation. It is right, therefore, that it should be the Government that sets the framework for the NHS and is held accountable in Parliament for the way that it operates. There must be a continuous thread of accountability through the system to the Government of the day; and it is for that reason that the Government believes that calls for an independent NHS board, which would remove the NHS from meaningful democratic control, are misplaced. Moreover, the NHS has just come through a period of re-organisation. We do not believe this is the right time to impose further top-down change to structures. What matters more is that there should always be clarity and transparency about who takes what decisions on our behalf. That is the assurance that the Constitution will provide.

13. The Constitution improves accountability by making clear:

- What individuals have a right to expect from the NHS

- The principles by which decisions will be made

- Who is responsible for what through a 'statement of accountability' to be published alongside the final version of the Constitution

7

14. We encourage PCTs to experiment with how they can improve the way they give and take account of local views, within the current legislative framework. Many PCTs are already doing this, working with local communities and partner organisations to come up with governance arrangements that increase their responsiveness in a way that best fits their local needs:

## Consultation process

15. The NHS belongs to us all. The Constitution is designed to reflect what matters, whether to patients, public or members of staff. It is therefore vital that the formal consultation builds on the process so far.

16. We will therefore create a Constitutional Advisory Forum that will bring together leading representatives from the patient, clinical and managerial communities, to oversee the consultation process. The Forum will work with the NHS to lead a process of engagement in every region of England, and report key messages back to the Secretary of State. It will be co-chaired by David Nicholson, the NHS Chief Executive, and Ivan Lewis, the sponsoring Minister.

# 8
# Implementation
Maintaining the momentum

An advanced practitioner assesses mammograms at the Nightingale Breast Screening Centre, Manchester

# 8

# Implementation
Maintaining the momentum

1. This Review has shown that there is enormous enthusiasm and energy throughout the NHS for achieving the vision set out in this report. The ambitious plans set out in every NHS region will be challenging to implement but in each case will improve services radically for patients.

2. I am keen that the pace should not drop. While change of this magnitude will not happen overnight, we should constantly strive to achieve high quality care for patients and the public. This chapter sets out how this will happen.

**Leading local change**

3. The Review as a whole has exemplified the process I believe will deliver these changes as effectively as possible. At its core has been the development of visions in every NHS region. We should now back local leaders – clinical and managerial – to deliver them.

4. I know that in each region, strategic health authorities (SHAs) are already working with primary care trusts (PCTs) to discuss proposals locally and ensure that the views of NHS staff, patients and the public are taken into account. In many cases change is already happening and patients are feeling the benefits.

5. By Spring 2009, each PCT will publish its strategic plan, setting out a five-year plan for improving the health of people locally. These plans will put into practice the evidence-based pathways of care at the heart of each region's vision. They will show a strong emphasis on partnership working between PCTs, local authorities and other partners (public, private and third sector – including social enterprise) to ensure that local health and wellbeing needs are better understood and addressed.

**Enabling local change**

6. Centrally, we will enable local improvements in three ways.

- First, we will ensure that the funding is there to deliver the changes. The Department of Health will later this year make financial allocations to every PCT for the next two years. This will give PCTs clarity about the money they have to invest in improving the health of their populations.

- Second, we will publish an NHS Operating Framework in October this year to set out the enabling system that will deliver this Review. Before then, the NHS Chief Executive and I will meet with staff across the NHS to discuss how to ensure this document best supports the delivery of PCT strategic plans.

8

- And third, we will ensure that, as
the Department of Health develops
the policy proposals described in
this report (via legislation, where
necessary), it does so in partnership
with the NHS and stakeholders to
ensure that the benefits we have
all identified are fully realised.
This will include Equality Impact
Assessment wherever appropriate.
Where a comprehensive evidence-
base does not yet exist, we will
also commission a programme of
independent evaluation to improve
learning and ensure transparency
and public accountability.[106]

## Conclusion

7. It has been a privilege to lead the
NHS Next Stage Review. I am
delighted that thousands of people
have taken part in the process and
have seized the opportunity to shape
an NHS fit for the 21st century.

8. The priorities they have identified,
together with the steps set out in this
final report, represent an ambitious
vision, one focused firmly on the
highest quality of care for patients
and the public. I challenge everyone
who works in and with the NHS to
deliver it for the benefit of this and
future generations.

106 This will achieve the goal of a close dialogue
between policy-makers and researchers
advocated in N. Black. Evidence based policy:
proceed with care. BMJ. 2001 Nov 17:323
(7322): 1187.

Printed in the UK by The Stationery Office Limited
on behalf of the Controller of Her Majesty's Stationery Office
ID5849435   07/08   404944   19585

Printed on Paper containing 75% recycled fibre content minimum.